T0266209

the MAN
BEHIND *the*
BATON

the MAN BEHIND the BATON

The Maestro, The Law, The Legend™

DR. WILLIAM PATRICK FOSTER

Published by Advantage, Charleston, South Carolina.
Member of Advantage Media Group.

ADVANTAGE is a registered trademark and the Advantage colophon is a trademark of Advantage Media Group, Inc.

Cover photo courtesy Florida Department of State Archives.

Printed in the United States of America.

ISBN: 978-1-59932-729-7
LCCN: 2016938617

Dr. William P. and Mary Ann Foster Foundation
P.O. Box 5393
Tallahassee, Florida 32314
www.drwpfosterfoundation.org
E-mail: info@drwpfosterfoundation.org

Advantage Media Group is proud to be a part of the Tree Neutral® program. Tree Neutral offsets the number of trees consumed in the production and printing of this book by taking proactive steps such as planting trees in direct proportion to the number of trees used to print books. To learn more about Tree Neutral, please visit **www.treeneutral.com**. To learn more about Advantage's commitment to being a responsible steward of the environment, please visit **www.advantagefamily.com/green**

Advantage Media Group is a publisher of business, self-improvement, and professional development books and online learning. We help entrepreneurs, business leaders, and professionals share their Stories, Passion, and Knowledge to help others Learn & Grow. Do you have a manuscript or book idea that you would like us to consider for publishing? Please visit **advantagefamily.com** or call **1.866.775.1696.**

To my beloved wife, Mary Ann Duncan Foster, for being a wonderful friend, confidante, helpmate, and supporter.

To my sons, William Patrick Foster, Jr. and Anthony Frederick Foster, for their love and support.

Dr. WILLIAM
PATRICK FOSTER

THE MAESTRO, THE LAW, THE LEGEND™

Tribute

It gives me great pleasure to provide this tribute to a man that has made an indelible impression in my world—my dad, Dr. William P. Foster. I affectionately refer to him as "Doc" because he always displayed the wisdom and right cure for any and all needs of our family. Often times the right cure was his abiding love, understanding, character, determination to never flinch in support for his family and the interest that he took in our growth and undertakings.

There is no question that "Doc" taught and showed me the meaning of hard work and also the resulting harvest. Each and every day he demonstrated the value of embracing your passion and then painting the world one stroke at a time with shear effort. Of course, music was his passion, and his unrelenting efforts wrought numerous coveted recognitions and awards including the Sudler Award and opportunities such as participation in the Bastille Day Parade, Super Bowls, and Inaugural celebrations. His example influenced my step into these shoes of passionate labor, and now I enjoy working with the The Dr. William P. and Mary Ann Foster Foundation on his behalf.

"Doc" was a drum major for education as the great equalizer. I am thankful for his insistence that this pathway be the means to ensure quality of life. "Doc" was adamant about good morals and character, and so I thank him for the man that I have become. "Doc" understood that a man's work is not complete until he also reaches out and makes valiant contributions that uplift his fellow man and community. I thank him for awakening me to this notion of duty and discharge. "Doc" subscribed to the need for spiritual nourishment, growth, and deliverance. I now find my days blessed and sustained as I have taken up the mantle of worship as initiated by my father.

The record speaks for itself and shows that "Doc" was an extraordinary composer, conductor, bandmaster, and Dad. History will reflect that he was the creator of the Florida A and M University Marching "100" Band and also a value system for which I will be eternally grateful. The community and the world will long remember his professional contributions, and I will forever remember his paternal love.

—Anthony F. Foster
member, Dr. William P. and Mary Ann Foster Foundation

Anthony F. Foster with his parents,
Mrs. Mary Ann Foster and Dr. William P. Foster

The Foster Family

From upper left: Anthony Frederick Foster, William Patrick Foster, Jr., Mary Ann Duncan Foster, and Dr. William P. Foster, Sr.

Dr. William Patrick Foster

The Maestro, The Law, The Legend

Table of Contents

Acknowledgments

The compilation and publication of this book was not a solo act. Many people have shaped its content. Thus, at the outset, I express my sincere and heartfelt gratitude to so many individuals.

Deep appreciation is expressed to all of the following people for their lifelong support: Dr. Vito Pascucci, chairman of the board and CEO of G. Leblanc Corporation, for philanthropic support and friendship for more than three decades; Dr. William H. Gray, Jr., Dr. George W. Gore, Jr., Dr. Benjamin L. Perry, Jr., Dr. Walter L. Smith, and Dr. Frederick S. Humphries, presidents and administrators of Florida Agricultural and Mechanical College and University, for the assistance and support during their respective administrations; the members of the 1946–1998 marching and symphonic bands, for their participation and contribution in rehearsals and performances from June 1, 1946–July 31, 1998; Dr. Inez Yergan Kaiser for support and assistance during the early and formative years (1950s and 1960s) to the Florida A&M College University Band Program, including sponsorship by Inez Kaiser and Associates.

Dr. Julian E. White, director of bands, Mr. Charles Bing, associate director of bands, and the students, faculty, and staff members of the FAMU Division of Bands and Department of Music from June 1, 1946–July 31, 1998, for their support and contributions to the program and operations of the university bands and the department of music.

Mr. Gaston O. Sanders (deceased), band director at Sumner High School, Kansas City, Kansas, for giving me the opportunity to serve as student director of the Sumner High School Band and Orchestra during 1935–1937. Mr. Sanders inspired me to pursue a career as a band director.

Mr. Edwin W. Peters (deceased), trumpet player, former member of the John Philip Sousa Band, Springfield, Missouri, for tutoring me on basic musicianship.

Dr. William D. Revelli (deceased), former director of bands, University of Michigan, my mentor and role model, for nominating me for the position of president of the American Bandmasters Association.

Dr. Paul V. Yoder, composer, arranger, and writer, for prompting me to write and submit my book, *Band Pageantry*, for publication by Hal Leonard Music, Inc., Winona, Minnesota, and Milwaukee, Wisconsin.

To my publishing team at Advantage Media Group, you provided the expertise and guidance necessary to make our vision a reality, and for that we are extremely grateful.

***

I want to express my utmost gratitude and sincerest appreciation to Thelma V. Crump for her unending support in making this book a success. For her work and sacrifice, I am forever grateful.

—Anthony F. Foster

Preface

My journey at Florida Agricultural and Mechanical University (also referred to as Florida A&M, FAMU, or—prior to 1953—Florida Agricultural and Mechanical College) began on June 1, 1946 as director of bands. A few years later I also became chairman of the FAMU Music Department. After fifty-two years of service, I stepped down from those duties on July 31, 1998. However, I remained on the teaching staff and was the holder of the Foster–Edmonds Endowed chair at FAMU until August 2001. My life's work has been exciting and fulfilling.

I appreciate so much the continuous support of FAMU students, faculty, staff, and administrators, as well as the sustained support of friends, businesses, and politicians. Everywhere I have gone, love has been shown to me. It's so good to be a Rattler.

Most of all, I appreciate the support of my wife, Mrs. Ann Foster, my best friend during the best of times and times of tribulations.

I am indebted to many throughout America and the world for the citations, hospitality, gifts, and other amenities bestowed upon my family and me. I have had many cordial and friendly receptions throughout the country. The heartwarming expressions of love shown to my wife and me through the years have deeply touched us. I have been truly overwhelmed by them.

Dr. William Patrick Foster

THE EARLY YEARS
THE BIRTH OF A SPECIAL CHILD

O nce in a great while, I'm told, a family welcomes into the fold, or into the household, a newborn offspring to whom they refer as a very special child. Some folks say that at my birth on August 25, 1919, in Kansas City, Kansas, my father, Mr. Frederick Bradford Foster, and my mother, Mrs. Venetia Highwarden-Foster, described me as a "special child." Well, while any son would welcome such a distinction, I cannot honestly attest to the authenticity or truth of such a designation. However, I can attest to the fact that my parents loved me and reared me, William Patrick Foster, in a loving and supportive manner.

William Patrick Foster

Whenever I reflect on past experiences, failures, and successes, I realize that I was blessed with very special parents and extended family. They provided me with the blessed and cherished heritage of an inspirational family who loved me enough to instill in me positive qualities. These qualities have not changed throughout the years.

William Patrick Foster

Frederick Bradford
Foster, father

Venetia Highwarden,
mother

My family took time to ground me in Christian training. My parents and grandparents taught me good manners; chastised me as needed; and taught me to give, receive, and appreciate love. They insisted that I honor and obey my parents, elders, and other people of authority—to respect ladies and gentlemen and honor and value all human beings (regardless of status or condition). They taught me to seek excellence and practice wholesome values and exemplary work ethic.

THE FAMILY TREE

I am often asked about my family tree. Some people want to know more about my family. It is not often that I take the time to talk about my childhood. It's not because I don't have fond memories of my childhood; in fact, just the opposite is true. I had a great childhood. However, since coming to Florida A&M University, my focus has been on my wife and children and my work. I suppose that in some ways, I am a very private person.

First, let me present some information about my family. Then, I will share the high points of my life's experiences with you. As you read about my family's tree, keep in mind that when I was growing up, the adults in the family did not give too much information to the children. When I was a child, I was told what the adult members of my family thought I needed to know. So I will give you as much information about the family as I can remember or find in records of that era.

Frederick Vondorus Foster and his wife

My father, Frederick Bradford Foster, was born in Carbondale, Kansas. He attended the University of Kansas during the 1904–1905 school year and then worked as a railway mail clerk.

He married my mother, Venetia

Highwarden, in 1906. My mother was born in Minneapolis, Minnesota.

My father and mother had four children: Frederick Vondorus Foster, Dorothy G. Foster, Delphos Leroy Foster, and me, William Patrick Foster.

Delphos Leroy Foster, Rosalie Lee Buckner, and their two children: Delphos Leroy Foster, Jr. and Dwight Foster

Dr. William P. Foster and Dorothy G. Foster

My brother, Vondorus Foster, was the oldest of the children. He had three wives: Alma, Evelena, and Ethel. Alma begat Betty Jane Foster. Evelena begat Gayle Patricia Foster. Ethel did not have a child.

Dorothy G. Foster was my only sister. She was married twice. Her first husband's family name was Spears, and her second husband's family name was Cotton. Dorothy did not have any children.

My brother, Delphos Leroy Foster, was married to Rosalie Lee Buckner. They had two children: Delphos Leroy Foster, Jr. and Dwight Foster.

My brothers, Vondorus and Delphos, and my sister, Dorothy Foster-Cotton, are deceased. All of these family members were born in Kansas City, Kansas.

Dr. William P. Foster with his wife, Mary Ann Duncan Foster, William Patrick Foster, Jr., and Anthony Frederick Foster

I am the youngest of the Foster children born to Frederick Bradford Foster and Venetia Highwarden-Foster.

I married a wonderful lady named Mary Ann Duncan. Mary Ann and I have two children.

Our older son is named William Patrick Foster, Jr. He is married to Patricia Drayton-Foster. William and Patricia have three children: William Patrick Foster, III, David Arnold Foster, and Kimberly Katherine Mary Ann Foster.

Anthony Frederick Foster, our younger son, has a daughter, Chesna Iman Foster.

William Patrick Foster, Jr., Patricia Drayton-Foster, William Patrick Foster, III, David Arnold Foster, and Kimberly Katherine Mary Ann Foster

MY MOTHER'S FAMILY

My mother's parents were Leroy Highwarden and Alice Williams-Highwarden. Leroy Highwarden and his brother operated a barbershop in Minneapolis, Minnesota.

After my mother's father, Leroy, died, her mother married William Washington Patrick. William Patrick was a good man and a great step-grandfather to me. I loved him. I stayed with him and Grandmother Alice most of the time when I was a child in Kansas City.

Anthony Foster

My mother's grandfather on her mother's side of the family was Augustus Williams. He was married to Aradna Williams. They were from Canada.

Leroy and Alice Highwarden moved their family to Kansas City, Kansas in 1894, when my mother was ten years old. Leroy and Alice had two daughters: Venetia and

Leroy Highwarden   Alice Williams-Highwarden

Ethel Highwarden. Venetia and Ethel attended the public schools in Kansas City, Kansas.

Ethel married Archie Gregg, a graduate of Kansas University and my father's friend. Mr. Gregg became president of Shorter College, a colored school in Little Rock, Arkansas. His brother, John A. Gregg, also a graduate of Kansas University, was an African Methodist Episcopal (AME) Church Bishop. Ethel and Archie are the parents of Archie and Ruth Gregg, who also graduated from Kansas University.

As a child I enjoyed and reaped the benefits of what I call extended-family hospitality during the time that my mother, two brothers, sister, and I lived with my grandparents in Kansas City. My grandfather and I developed a close bond, especially on those occasions when he allowed me the privilege of meeting him at the streetcar as he returned home from work every day. He would let me carry his lunch bucket to the house on weekdays. Understandably, those actions were big accomplishments for a small boy on his way to becoming a man—well, at least in my mind.

MY FATHER'S FAMILY

My father's father was named William Munson Foster. His wife (my father's mother) was named Laura Ann Ransom-Foster.

William Munson Foster was born in 1858, in Raleigh, North Carolina. His parents were slaves. William was married twice. In 1881, he married a Topeka girl, Lulu Odell. Lulu died two years into the marriage. William and Lulu had two sons. One of their children died in infancy. The other son, William, died in his thirties.

After the death of his first wife, Lulu, my paternal grandfather married another girl from Topeka, Laura Ann Ransom. Laura Ann was born in 1865 and married at nineteen years of age. She and Grandfather William had eleven children. All of them attended high school, and some of them went to college. William died in 1932. Laura Ann passed in 1948.

My father's maternal grandfather (Laura Ann Ransom-Foster's father) was an undertaker ("Undertaker" Ransom). His wife's name was Ann Ransom.

My father's grandmother, Ann Ransom, was the daughter of a slave woman and the slave master. The slave master was of Irish heritage. My father's grandmother, Ann Ransom, whom some called Grannie Ransom, looked like an Irishwoman: keen features, brown hair, and light-brown eyes. Ann Ransom was the mother of six children. They all lived in Topeka, except Annie, who lived in Denver, Colorado.

The Ransom family (the family of Grandmother Laura Ann Ransom-Foster) was one of the Exoduster families from Tennessee. They settled in Tennessee Town.

Grandfather William Munson Foster was a good provider; however, he liked to spend money. In contrast, Grandmother Laura Ann was quiet and thrifty. She tried to keep my grandfather's spending at a minimal level but was not very successful. If he had listened to his wife, he would have been a wealthy farmer instead of a "good liver."

The family was taught that owning property, getting a good education, and being in the political arena were very important but that "the family" was extremely important. However, our family style of interaction was not highly emotional. It was more business-like, impersonal, and functional. Money was important. Thus, we were taught that education provided a means of emancipation so that one would not be a burden on the family or society.

Also, religion was very important in our family life. There was a close spiritual relationship with God. We read the Bible and prayed. However, we have a variety of religious persuasions among the members of the Foster and Ransom families. No problem has ever presented itself.

Grandfather Foster was really not a slave, but his mother was. He was hired out at age seven and was legally bound to his former slave owner who took an oath to educate him. Instead of sending him to school, the man had his daughters attempt to teach him. Grandfather pretended that he was unable to learn, although later he learned to read and write.

Grandfather Foster worked hard and took his money home to his mother to help with the other children. At fourteen years of age he went to work on the railroad, saved his money, and helped his mother build a house. He hewed the logs and did all the work himself. He bought lasts and leather and made shoes for his brothers and sisters who had none. When he was sixteen years old, his mother and her five other children moved to Akron, Ohio. They left three children who were large enough to fend for themselves in North Carolina. The family never again heard from the children left behind. Grandfather Foster's mother died in Ohio, and in 1878 William Dalton, an Ohio farmer, brought my young grandfather to Topeka.

Grandfather Foster was a true Kansas pioneer, having helped build the statehouse, lay the first asphalt paving on the capital city's main street (Kansas Avenue), and construct its first waterworks plant. He was a foreman and received a dollar and a half a day. All the time he was working, he saved his money, and eventually he bought a farm near Carbondale where he lived for over fifty years.

My grandfather, who was part Cherokee Indian, was of medium build and was about six feet in height. An astute businessperson, he was the owner of a number of pieces of property and a small farm. He was employed by Union Pacific Railroad in the capacity of a courier mailman and watchman on the 8:00 a.m. to 5:00 p.m. shift. This was the only employment he had from his days as a young man until his retirement. Somehow, despite his obligations, he managed to establish a college savings account in my name.

During my grandfather's life span, I had access to an annual Union Pacific Railroad Pass, which allowed me to travel throughout the land without charge. I accompanied my grandfather and grand-mother on trips to Omaha, Nebraska, for an Indian-nation pow-wow and to Salt Lake City, Utah, for a Union Pacific Old-Timers Convention. I remember walking in the parade in Salt Lake City, touring the Mormon Tabernacle, and going to the beach of Salt Lake. I recall hearing that because the water contained a considerable amount of salt, a person could not drown in Salt Lake.

During the spring and summer vegetable-growing seasons, I accompanied my grandfather to a farm plot to till the soil, plant seeds, and water and harvest the crop. As usual, I thoroughly enjoyed working with and learning from my grandfather.

BACKGROUND

Kansas became a haven for multicultural groups of Black, Cherokee Indian, and White. They sought refuge in Kansas after their freedom had been violated. For African American ancestors, the violation occurred when they were taken as slaves. For the Native American ancestors, freedom was violated when their land was taken from them by chicanery and force. Indian ancestors came to Kansas during what is referred to, historically, as the "removal." These Indians were forced out of their land and sent to Indian Territory, which originally included present-day Kansas. The Western Cherokee tribes already occupied Kansas. Inhumane and bloody events occurred in the early 1800s. There was a government roundup after treaties were broken, and all appeals from the Indians failed.

It was with great risk that the Blacks left the South and came North after the emancipation. The White Southerners were faced with the possibility of losing their Black labor. They refused to believe the movement was serious, that their Blacks would want to leave them. As more and more Blacks left, resentment gave way to anger and threats. Still, Blacks continued to depart. Many White Southerners resorted to violence by beatings, molestations, and hangings. Black leaders were accosted and murdered by nightriders. Some Blacks favored migration to parts of the United States, while others went to Liberia.

Blacks had been going to Kansas even before the exodus of the late 1870s. Many were skilled in farming and rural living. Some suffered greatly from the harsh and cold Kansas weather.

IN SUMMARY

As we "men" of the family matured, my participation in our meetings took on more sophistication. We held lengthy, insightful conversations and discussions on a wide range of important subjects and news issues of the day. Even today I'm proud to say that those one to two hours of "manly" discourse greatly affected the true man I was to later become.

As our practical and intellectual base grew, my grandfather recognized the need for my educational experiences to expand accordingly.

Thus, he began to map out travel excursions for the two of us. Our trips spanned many miles from Kansas City to Omaha, from Salt Lake City to Carbondale and Topeka.

All along the way, my grandfather did not miss an opportunity to afford me travel-oriented lessons based in academics and in life. What better ways were there for me to learn to recognize, value, and appreciate the vast array of educational benefits inherent through guided travel? Truly, my grandfather was a man ahead of his time, a man among men.

Similarly, during our non-travel times, my extended family members were careful to make the best possible use of our years together—my formative years—which were well supervised, I might add. It was during those years that I was given regular and full doses of values or ethical training that I later found to be crucial, even mandatory to successful manhood. My folks felt that one could never have too much training in these areas, and God forbid that I should have too little. I knew that complaining or resisting would be futile. Thus, I cooperated willingly and fully.

Education

As the years and I grew, so did my home, church, community and formal training. In fact it expanded rapidly, sometimes too rapidly for me. I used to console myself with the thought that the home training was the only activity that continued around the clock. Luckily, the other developmental experiences and training activities ceased after a brief period of time. For example, in church, how long could a preacher preach? Or better still, how much preaching would the congregation tolerate in a service? The same applies to community activities. How long would volunteers in charge work for a mere pittance or for free? How long would dedication flourish?

My Mother and Stepfather

Being committed Christians themselves, my family reared me through Sunday school, church, Bible study, and prayer meetings. I went to church every Sunday with my grandmother at the First African Methodist Episcopal Church, but I do not recall any formal ceremony to accept their belief. I listened attentively (through no choice of my own), asked questions, learned a lot, believed what I was taught, and consciously practiced (and sometimes dramatized) what I both saw and learned in church. I believed in God and in Jesus Christ, His Son.

Yet, I must admit that the spiritual grounding I received as a trusting youth has made and continues to make a decided difference in all aspects of my life. In addition to other roles, the church played the roles of spiritual re-enforcer of the values that were instilled in me at home and the self-appointed enforcer of its own rules or code of conduct. I can truthfully say that my personality resulted from the influences of others in my family and from all the things that happened in that environment at the time.

Again, in terms of community experiences, as was true of many youth of my day, I accepted and benefited from the few community activities that were available. I particularly liked playing basketball, horseshoes, baseball, and touch football. Through the interrelatedness of home, church, and community endeavors, the formula or outline for what was to become my philosophy of life began to emerge. Unorganized and organized, unsupervised and supervised community activities helped fine-tune me for the symphonies I was to later conceive, play, and demonstrate in my career.

Building upon my earlier experiences, community activities helped me learn to be an independent and a group learner, to work successfully as an individual, and to perform equally effectively as a team player. It

My step-grandfather

was at this stage of my development that I was encouraged to do many useful things: adopt a positive outlook on life, develop confidence in my abilities, value good interpersonal skills, complete tasks begun, respect the rights and opinions of others, embrace good character, be a team player, and aspire to be a leader who respected and honors his peers, etc.

As fate would have it, however, during those early years, I continued to learn that my composite education was never fully in my hands. Realizing that, I resolved to learn all I could at every opportunity from every available source. Again, my doing so was a tremendous resolve that has served me well.

Stowe Elementary School basketball team, 1930, with William P. Foster, standing fifth from the right

While attending Keeling Elementary School in first through third grades, my time was divided between the home of my stepfather and my mother, Mr. and Mrs. William Riley Tucker, at 359 Troupe Avenue, and the home of my step-grandfather and my grandmother, Mr. and Mrs. William Washington Patrick, at 410 Quindaro Boulevard. (It was from my step-grandfather that I acquired my given name, William Patrick.) The Keeling Elementary School was halfway between these two homes, a distance of only three blocks. Therefore, I had the best of both worlds, so to speak.

Although I looked forward to attending school each day, I waited anxiously for lunch break so I could taste the goodies hidden in the brown lunch bag I carried to school every day. Unfortunately, few modern-day elementary students will ever realize what comfort and delight such brown-bag fringe benefits gave to my friends and me.

Having achieved much through the instruction at Keeling, I progressed to Harriett Beecher Stowe Elementary School for fourth-, fifth-, and sixth-grade instruction. Stowe Elementary was located one block south of Third Street on Richmond Avenue, just six blocks from my mother's home. So, again, I felt that God had smiled on me.

From 1931–1934, expanding my horizons (or should I say flexing my muscles?), I was a member of the fifth- and sixth-grade basketball team at Stowe Elementary School where we played in an elementary school basketball league.

Since my mother's home was across the street from Northeast Junior High School, I enjoyed numerous evening and weekend hours playing basketball, baseball, and football on the school playground.

Still trying my wings, marching to my own beat, or ensuring my physical endurance, I became a newspaper carrier of three newspapers: the *Kansas City Call* (a Black paper), the *Kansas City Kansan*, and *Kansas City Times Star* (general papers). In addition I worked as a filling station attendant, as a drug store clerk, and as a "drugstore cowboy" (bicycle delivery boy)—minus the boots, spurs, and gun, however.

And the melodious, steady tune continued to play on the back roads of my mind, as time and activity progressed.

As I sit here more than seventy years later, I can still visualize my old middle-school structure. In vivid images, metaphors especially, I can see, hear, and feel the inseparability and closeness of my grand-father and me. Truly, as Natalie Cole sings, "We were inseparable."

Suffice it to say that my grandfather took up a considerable amount of time with me every evening. He continued to urge me to academic excellence, to venture out, and even to risk failure, if necessary. Yes, and to court success at every opportunity, too!

In later years as a member of the Northeast Junior High School track team, I was awarded the Northeast Letter for running the 440-yard race. It was during my junior high years, also, that I learned tennis and became an accomplished player. (Looking back, I wonder if I could have been an Arthur Ashe.)

I guess you could say that by this time in my junior high career, I was wide open! At least I know that I was not doing what some students today refer to as "chilling." In contrast, I wanted to learn everything! To participate in everything!

I enjoyed playing horseshoe games during the summer months. I learned to play and enjoy whist, hearts, and bridge, as only my mother could teach them. Of course, during junior high, I worked hard to earn good grades; to be an exemplary student; and to make my parents, stepparents, and grandparents proud of me. I took my assignments seriously and tried to fulfill all requirements as the adults in my life expected.

Although my teachers were serious disciplinarians, they were also comforting, inspiring nurturers and facilitators. They believed in my classmates and me and in our innate abilities. They saw our potential, uncovered our talents, and aroused our interests.

It was during this formative period that I continued my self-employment ventures—mowing lawns, pruning shrubs, raking lawns, and washing and polishing automobiles. (Perhaps I could have been a businessman or a corporate executive?)

Anyway, unlike many enterprises today, my self-employment "business" flourished. From my initial savings account I purchased a C Melody Saxophone that cost around fifty dollars back in that day.

Afterward, I attended the Horner Institute of Music in Kansas City, Missouri, for instructional lessons. The Italian teacher, unaware of my tremendous personal accomplishment in having even obtained an instrument, informed me that the C melody saxophone was obsolete. He suggested that I purchase a B-flat clarinet before returning for lessons. Although pained and disappointed, I took his advice.

Thus began the preparation for my career as a musician. Some say the rest is history: William P. Foster history. I don't know about that, but certainly, I am grateful for all of my experiences and opportunities.

Subsequently, I joined the Northeast Junior High clarinet class and the school band. This action led to my becoming a member of the Sumner High School Band, upon entering Sumner High School for tenth-, eleventh-, and twelfth-grade instruction. Because of my fast progress as a performer on the clarinet, Mr. Gaston O. Sanders, director of the Sumner High School Band and Orchestra, appointed me student director of the band and orchestra. He taught me to play the violoncello and allowed me to play in the Sumner High School Orchestra. Understandably, I was greatly honored.

It was my good fortune to tune and direct the high school band and orchestra each day for three years (1934–1937). I continued to enroll and be productive in industrial arts classes in the area of woodworking. I recall having made several items, among them being a large ottoman, a tie rack, a telephone stand, and other household furniture.

Clearly, industrial-arts classes were favorites of mine. Other favorites were band, orchestra, geometry, physics, mathematics, and mechanical arts (drawing)—a strange mix of disciplines, some people think. Yet, their perceived strangeness does not end with those courses, because I enjoyed theatre and drama courses as well. Often, I played various roles in campus productions.

Further, during my high school years I helped my grandfather with his position as caretaker and custodian of the Masonic Lodge Building, located on the second top-floor at Fifth and Washington Boulevard in Kansas City. The chores included scrubbing the wood floors, cleaning the windows, dusting and polishing the furniture, sweeping the stairwell, and cleaning the restroom. Clearly, my family and my circumstances teamed up to ensure that I moved to the invigorating tunes of sustained physical agility as often and as fully as possible. Perhaps they had a view of the future I had not seen.

Apparently, my family, church, and community members knew what work-related challenges would await me when as a young "professional-to-be" I would become employed as a teacher and band director at Lincoln High School in Springfield, Missouri. Although I would never have dreamed of those initial and other soon-to-follow professional periods of my career as "Pre-FAMU Years," I now recognize them as such.

Being a workaholic who was perpetually full of energy and being a positive thinker, I was not by any means discouraged or fearful. I just jumped right in, poised to meet each challenge or obstacle boldly. I was determined to succeed. In fact I had to succeed. There was no alternative. I had vowed to be successful. All of my ancestors, immediate and historical, had claimed my success. I had to make the grade.

Repeatedly, I whispered to myself, "Pat, there's no time for discordant notes, short practices, or early dismissals. You can't get caught up in reasons for not performing and excuses for failing. Excuses please no one but their maker." Thus, I learned to weather the storms.

BACHELOR'S DEGREE

The period of 1937–1941 represents my continued developmental years into manhood, but this was also the time that I was a student at the University of Kansas. Because of limited financial resources, I sought employment as a waiter in the sorority and fraternity houses. I worked six hours every day in exchange for lodging and boarding in the basement of the sorority or fraternity house, plus a stipend of three to four dollars each week. (One could say I was a man of means, right?)

I had to compete in the classroom with the same students to whom I served breakfast, lunch, and dinner on a daily basis. However, since I was aware of the times and circumstances, I did not despair. I knew about discrimination, unfairness, and dejection. I was not about to let those things stop me from attaining my education. Knowing that my situation was temporary and, as the popular saying goes, "This, too, shall pass," I stayed quietly but thoughtfully and determinedly on course.

Because of strict segregation at the university, I could not attend any of the social functions on the weekends and could only have meals in one table area reserved for colored students in the student-union building. Notwithstanding this, the quality of educational instruction and training in the classroom was excellent. I received a top education that permitted me to compete at the university and in life itself on the highest level with anyone. I am thankful for the training and education I received at the University of Kansas.

Certainly, my undergraduate days, weeks, and years were busy ones. For what seemed like the longest time, during the entire school week, I utilized free blocks of time to perfect clarinet exercises, practice on the piano, study for classes, and complete music-theory assignments. Every weekday night I used the 7:00 p.m.-11:00 p.m. blocks of time to study or to practice on the clarinet and the piano. On Saturdays and Sundays,

William P. Foster from the 1941 Jayhawker Yearbook

I practiced on the clarinet or piano and studied academic subjects during the mornings, afternoons, and evenings. By maintaining that vigorous schedule, I was able to make up, academically, for the time I spent waiting tables at the sorority and fraternity houses.

During my first two years of college at the University of Kansas, from 1937 until my grandfather's death in 1939, I made frequent trips on weekends to Kansas City, Kansas, to take my clothes home to my mother for washing and pressing, as well as to enjoy long visits with my grandfather. After his death, however, as was to be expected, going home was never the same for me. Also, going home was not as easy, since I no longer had use of the Union Pacific Annual Pass. Looking back, I realize that although I lost my dearest friend, I experienced some degree of closure to a wonderful era of my life. Today, even after more than sixty years, I still miss my grandfather dearly and continue to understand that although his death was a great loss to me in many ways, his life was of immeasurable value.

Periodically, my social life at the university included going to concerts, sports events, and social affairs at the colored fraternity or sorority houses. However, most of my time at the university continued to be used for classes, work, or study. My main focus was on the business at hand, with very limited time for pleasure.

One day, as graduation time approached, I don't know what possessed me to go to my dean's office—but while I was there, he asked what I planned to do after graduating from the University of Kansas. I replied that I planned and wished to become a conductor. He responded that I might give more thought to that plan because there were no job openings or opportunities for colored conductors. That unexpected answer, which stunned me for a moment, became the catalyst that instilled within me a deep commitment to disprove his assertion, while fully and emphatically realizing my dreams, despite his admonition and despite any odds.

MASTER'S DEGREE

During the summers of 1947, 1948, 1949, and 1950, I enrolled at Wayne State University to pursue the master of arts degree in music. The date of my graduation was August 1950.

My education and training at Wayne State University opened up a new horizon in my career. While there, I was fortunate enough to have an in-service experience in radio and television, the latter of which was in its embryonic developmental stage. Television was a new medium then. Now, it is one that dominates the media of communication and visual/audio presentations over the airways.

The pragmatic training and experience at Wayne State University were of immense value to me, as I was once director of a weekly radio program at Florida A&M College. I took from Wayne State University a cadre of information and techniques to experiment with in developing the weekly radio program, beamed from Lee Hall Auditorium at Florida A&M College.

I also began to understand the possibilities of television and how I could apply production techniques to band pageantry, marching band, pre-game, and halftime shows.

DOCTORAL DEGREE

I was the recipient of a Rockefeller General Education Board Fellowship to study toward a doctoral degree at Teachers College, Columbia University, for the period of September 1953 to May 1954 and January 1955 to May 1955.

New York City was an unparalleled learning laboratory for me. While in the doctoral program, I was a resident of International House for lodging and boarding. The music room at International House was an excellent facility for me to use in listening to phonograph recordings of all periods, from baroque through contemporary. I became quite proficient about four weeks before the doctoral-qualifying music-listening examination. The person administering the examination played four to six phonograph records and required me to write specific responses relevant to the period of the music, which consisted of naming the composition and providing an analytical resume of the music to include the form and characteristics of the music.

Other segments of the doctoral-qualifying examination included music theory, the writing of an essay, education principles, and philosophy with special emphasis on principles of music education.

At either no cost or only a minimum fee, I was afforded an opportunity to attend orchestra performances, choral-ensemble, and solo concerts and recitals, as well as Metropolitan Opera performances.

I was one of the students selected to sit in on rehearsals of the New York Philharmonic Orchestra. Music scores were accessible for both orchestra and opera performances. In addition to the opportunity of studying with world-renowned faculty, my association with outstanding graduate students was awe inspiring, highly motivating, and stimulating.

These experiences made me feel that I was on the cutting edge of the entire spectrum of music and music education.

As holder of the Rockefeller General Education Board Fellowship, I served as guest professor, lecturing to instrumental classes at Teachers College, Columbia University, and was included in faculty meetings and social affairs with adjunct professors and other fellowship holders.

New York City was a great developmental laboratory for me. The things I learned at Teachers College, Columbia University enhanced my career as an administrator, educator, and conductor.

Courtship and Marriage

People have often said to me that any time a loving marriage has not only lasted but also has flourished for sixty-two years, certainly, something magical must have begun during the courtship period and remained constant throughout the union. Even today, others say that indeed such a marriage must be the result of a miracle.

Well, I can accept both of these assessments. I believe in both magic and miracles. In fact, I have experienced—and continue to experience—them with the love of my life. My wife is my precious God-given gift, my lover, friend, confidante, helpmate, and fan club. She is the mother of our children, the grandmother of our grandchildren, and the great-grandmother of our great-grandchildren.

Mary Ann Duncan

I've heard that some "marriages are made in Heaven." If this is true, I think that ours qualifies for that distinction, since it has always been "for better" and never "for worse." It seems that from the day I met that very special lady named Mary Ann Duncan, I loved her. Does that sound like the unbelievable "love at first sight" affliction? A love-at-first-sight feeling that could be nurtured year after year, despite life's episodes, decisions, challenges, and changes? Well, admittedly, it was—except that the affliction was positive and the love was—and is—real!

My relationship with Mary Ann began when I was a student at the University of Kansas. I thought she was a very beautiful young lady when we first met, and I later learned that her inner and outer qualities combined to make her the most beautiful woman in the world—certainly in my world. Luckily for me, she and her parents lived near me, and I made sure she had ample opportunities to see me pass by her house. On our first date, we went to a movie. I don't remember, but Mary Ann says we didn't talk much. What do you think must have gotten into me?

I can recall the initial action I took to begin dating Mary Ann. (It was an action that I would not recommend to young men in today's explosive environment.) At the time, Mary Ann was friendly with a neighbor who lived two doors from her home. However, not to be deterred, (though perhaps a little foolish) on that fateful day when I saw Mary Ann and her friend conversing quietly at her home in Kansas City, I simply walked up to them, courteously addressed the young man, and asked his permission to take Mary Ann out. Surprisingly, he honored my request.

Since Mary Ann and her family were acquainted with me as a "good" neighborhood young man—as a young college student trying to make something of himself—they did not give me any trouble or resistance. Surely, I was happy about that. Mary Ann was a high school junior, and I was already in college. You can understand how such a relationship could have created much resistance. I'm glad I lived in the right neighborhood and on the right block. I'm also glad that I was a college student.

Mary Ann and I enjoyed a brief relationship as a young couple getting to know each other and our families better. We learned to talk more, to be comfortable in each other's company, and to "foster" mutual trust. After having dated for a couple of months, Mary Ann and I decided to get married. I guess you could say we eloped. Once we agreed to marry, without notifying anyone, we drove to Olathe, Kansas, about twenty miles from Kansas City. On August 8, 1939 Mary Ann and I took our wedding vows at the courthouse. Then, we drove home and went to dinner. Afterward, my bride and I partook of a little "social repass" and notified our families of our marriage. That was quite a day! Both of our families were surprised that we had eloped, but everyone took our news in stride. My wife and I began our new life together at my parents' home.

My wife and I are thankful for that young friend of hers for his chivalrous acquiescence. We thank God for each other and our abiding love. Truly, we have been delightfully happy and satisfied with each other and are glad we eloped.

Although she did not work before coming with me to Florida Agricultural and Mechanical College (FAMC), my wife decided to do so once we got settled in Tallahassee, Florida. She thoroughly enjoyed being around, assisting, inspiring, and advising FAMC students. Mary Ann provided such services to students for many years.

Mary Ann retired as office manager for the Student Activities Office (a job she loved) at Florida A&M in 1987. Professionally trained as an X-ray technician, she worked closely with volumes of students for many years prior to her retirement. The plaque she was presented with at her retirement dinner reads:

"She is the student's friend, mother, sister, brother, father, even a doctor, counselor, mentor, and a superior teacher. She simply did it all. She is the Director's Chief Assistant, Office Manager, Outstanding Administrator, Super Typist, Ardent Advisor, Attentive Listener, and an Absolute Friend. She is charming, neat, and has a great sense of humor. She is perceptive and giving. But most of all, she is a success! She is a dynamic leader, a caring secretary, and a great humanitarian. She is Student Activities."

I thank God for the wonderful wife he gave me. I thank that former friend, too. I hope that he found a wife as special as mine. More importantly, however, I hope that I have been as great a husband to Mary Ann as she has been a wife to me.

Asked by my editor to name two of the most exciting, gratifying, or relaxing aspects of our marriage, my wife replied, "We are still with each other after all of these years." Responding to a second query, "What would you say is Dr. Foster's most beautiful attribute?" my wife said, "Whatever I want, he will see that I get." I think that's pretty good, don't you? As long as I live, I'll never stop doing just that. After all, Mary Ann answered yes to both my dating and marriage proposals. That answer has made all the difference in my life. I shall forever cherish and be grateful to her. I could not have earned the success we enjoy had it not been for my wife's support.

My immediate family consists of my wife, Mary Ann Foster, and two sons. William P. Foster, Jr., a retired physicist at Bethesda Naval Research Center, and his wife, Patricia Drayton Foster, principal at Francis Key Middle School, reside in Silver Spring, Maryland. William and Patricia have three children: William P. Foster, III, David Arnold Foster, and Kimberly Mary Ann Foster. William is a jazz electric bassist and professional musician. Kimberly Katherine Mary Ann Foster, a teacher in Prince George County, Maryland, is married to Eric Wilson, an assistant principal in Silver Spring. They have two children: Cortney, a daughter, and Alan Wilson, their son.

Anthony Frederick Foster, my younger son, lives in New York City and works as a teacher with the New York City Board of Education. He has a daughter, Chesna Iman Foster.

The Pre-FAMC Years

DR. WILLIAM P. FOSTER: 1941–1946

Increasingly, I realize that my family, church, and community members must have known that mind-boggling challenges would await me when, as an aspiring professional, I became employed as a teacher and band director, first at a high school, and later at three colleges.

Immediately upon my arrival in 1941 at Lincoln High School in Springfield, Missouri (where I would stay until 1943), I knew that I did not have to write home for an assessment of the magnitude of my job responsibilities. (However, certainly, I would have welcomed and could have benefited greatly from a family-written instructional manual, which might have been appropriately titled, "A Blueprint for Success, Despite the Odds.")

Being a person dedicated to marching to the beat of the drummer constantly playing on the band fields of my mind, I thought, "I'll just have to call upon all that I have been taught, mentally and spiritually, as well as physically." With this determination, I raised my baton, signaling for anyone to see—and perhaps, more significantly, for myself to believe that I was ready for the challenges and would meet each one, in the precise order in which they occurred.

"In fact," I spoke aloud, "I'll meet them second by second, minute by minute, hour by hour, day by day, week by week, month by month, and even year by year." With baton raised and mind determined, I positioned myself for eventual success, a goal I would pursue by any sacrifices necessary.

As a teacher at Lincoln High School, I had to convince myself of this daily. I learned that not only did I have to woo or court adversity but also I had to fine-tune my technique of humming a tune while doing so. Definitely, humming was a plus in that it helped to sustain me during the long hours of necessary drudgery. It even put a bit of "pep in my step" and "glide in my stride," as students sometimes say.

During my ensuing work at Lincoln High School, I had no inkling that one day I would think of that period of service as the beginning of what I now refer to as "The Pre-FAMU Years." I am grateful for that service, however, for as you will learn later, it prepared me for the numerous challenges I eventually faced as my career expanded.

I was employed by the Springfield, Missouri Board of Education as teacher of music and as director of a mixed choir—later identified as an a cappella choir. Also, I was hired as director of band and director of bot h the boys' and the girls' glee clubs.

My initial challenge was to recruit personnel for each of the musical organizations. It was my good fortune to have the social studies teacher volunteer her services as piano accompanist for the seventy-voice a cappella choir, the girls' glee club and the boys' glee club. She was relieved of two academic classes to serve as accompanist for the choir that met three times each week and the two glee clubs that met twice each week.

Since the first obstacle was to encourage students and parents to purchase band instruments, the relatives and friends of students at Lincoln were encouraged to purchase used instruments from pawnshops and music stores. During free periods or study classes, students were invited to come to my studio-office for instruction in playing their instruments. I gave instruction to homogeneous and heterogeneous instrument classes. The band class period was one big applied music lesson. Instruction books consisted of scales and technique books, chorales, and *Bennett Band Book No. 1*.

The principal of Lincoln High School was Mr. Houston. He gave his full support to the music program. Since no specific facilities or rooms were designated in which the music groups could rehearse, I received permission for the choral groups to rehearse in an assigned classroom and for the band, which was organized from scratch, to meet in the auditorium/gymnasium. Folding chairs were used on the floor area of the combined auditorium/gymnasium.

During this period of public-school education in America, very few schools' organizations were fortunate enough to have budgets for their operations. To the best of my knowledge, the support of the music organizations came through lunchroom/cafeteria receipts. In addition, several appeals for financial assistance were made to parents, organizations and individuals, both within and outside of the school: the principal, faculty members, parent-teacher associations, community groups, and various other individuals.

On occasion, when the seventy-voice a cappella choir and glee clubs presented seasonal concerts at churches in Springfield and at Lincoln High School, the music performances gained enthusiastic responses. Wonderful backing for the various music programs followed. The diverse groups were often invited to perform in concert and on special community programs.

A lot of excitement and pride came in the form of a formal invitation for the choir to participate on a local radio program. The choir performed joyfully and admirably. It received many accolades. Joy broke again when the choir received its most significant honor: an invitation to perform at a concert in convention sessions of the Missouri State Educators Association in St. Louis, Missouri. Again, the choir received a rousing response from conferees and rave reviews from the Springfield, Missouri, community upon our "triumphant" return.

Oddly enough, just as positive, complimentary, and supportive reactions to the music program that I had labored so hard to build, stabilize, and enhance began to come to fruition, I realized that my time to depart Lincoln High School had come. As we say, "All good things must end." Of course, as music teacher and aspiring band director, I left with mixed feelings. Humbly, I was proud of my music students' accomplishments and wanted to be a part of their continued growth and development. Yet, according to the Good Book, "There's a time for everything." That was the time for me to continue to pursue my dream of becoming a successful band director—and, of course, of building a colored band that was second to none in the country. I just prayed that my genuine efforts, encouragement, and support had made a significant difference for the school and the community.

So it was with my tenure at Lincoln High School when in May 1943, my wife, son, and I departed Springfield, Missouri, and returned to Kansas City, Kansas, to seek greater challenges and personal development. The stepping-stone opportunity came to me during the 1943 summer period from Dr. Horace Mann Bond, president of Fort Valley State College, Fort Valley, Georgia.

In August 1943, I agreed to accept a threefold assignment: chairman, Department of Music; director, Fort Valley State Choir; and assistant professor, Music Education. Some people would say I had arrived. Others would believe that I had a free ticket to success. As you can quickly ascertain, the truth is that, again, my work was cut out for me. But, as usual, I welcomed the challenge. As you recall, challenges fire me up and make my adrenaline flow.

After having been cordially met at the train station late at night in Fort Valley, Georgia, by a member of the maintenance staff, I was taken to my temporary housing quarters. The following morning I was directed to my "musically-endowed" headquarters: a small demonstration house for students in home economics. Later, I was situated in a small house where I learned to "make do."

The following morning, I received keys to my office, located in the academic building. The building housed classrooms and faculty offices. My assigned office could have been labeled "office limited" because of its limited size, furniture, facilities, and equipment (no telephone, typewriter, copy machine, piano, table, etc.).

My earlier exuberance upon hearing about the academic building soon subsided as I realized that indeed I was in a dismal situation. Again, I would have welcomed some practical assistance. I felt a need to go back to my residence (my home economics residence) and commence to read my imagined family manual, "A Blueprint for Success, Despite the Odds."

Anyway, eventually I concluded that time either softens the blow or numbs the feeling so that one can function. And function I learned to do! As I mentioned before, I had no choice. I had to just do it.

The first music-related blow I immediately implored time to soften was my finding that because World War II was in operation, few male students were attending Fort Valley College. The second was my learning that I was one of only two music faculty members. The only other teacher was a young lady who taught piano, voice, and public-school music courses, in addition to serving as piano accompanist for the college choir, which was composed of all women. "There's that limited feature, again," I sighed. Accordingly, my teaching assignment was limited to serving as director of the female choir and to expounding instructional fundamentals of music to elementary-education majors.

However, the college choir I directed was quite active in performing at weekly college assemblies, concert presentations in neighboring cities, and concert tours in the state of Georgia.

To some extent, success and support in those activities helped numb my original feelings of despair and thereby rendered me capable of providing a quality service and being my usual optimistic self.

One of the most rewarding college events that I experienced was the Fort Valley State College folk-music festival. It drew talented folk singers and musicians from throughout the State of Georgia to a three-day music festival on campus. The event provided me with my initial opportunity to hear and appreciate raw primitive folk music via instrumentalists, vocalists, soloists, duets, trios, and quartets. Many of the participants played beautifully and masterfully on personally homemade string and percussion instruments.

I probably gained more than some students. Definitely, those non-college- or non-university-trained musicians were unusual—uniquely and fully skilled. Simply put, they were spectacular. Throughout their myriad performances, I kept exclaiming quietly to myself (at least I *think* it was quietly), "Gracious! What talent, what skill, what presence!"

The fine array of instruments included all types of homemade string instruments, e.g., violins, guitars, banjos, bass violins, and all types and forms of homemade percussion instruments, including tom-toms, snare drums, bongos, xylophones, and other crudely fashioned percussion instruments.

Definitely, the folk-music festival held in the spring of 1943-44 was an experience, both enjoyable and memorable! That singular event raised me to a new level of exuberance, a level I needed severely. At the time, I was beginning to feel that nothing could be sweeter, except for the arrival of my wife and Pat, Jr., of course. I thought of an old Jackie Gleason exclamation: "How sweet it is!" In September 1943, Ann and Pat, Jr. joined me, and my life was complete. Gleason had it right.

Ann and I were blessed with the birth of our second son, Anthony Frederick Foster, on April 28, 1944. Appropriately, Anthony was born in the Fort Valley State College Infirmary, increasing the family to four members.

In reflection, several pleasant memories relevant to our tenure at Fort Valley State present themselves. One of the usual features we enjoyed was that of families dining together for breakfast, lunch, and dinner. The fact that all meals were family-style was a real plus. My family and I enjoyed our one-year residence at Fort Valley State College and in Fort Valley, Georgia. Our stay was enjoyable because of the friendliness of the people, especially by Fort Valley State College administrators, faculty, staff, and definitely by the students we grew to love so dearly. We returned to Kansas City in time for the summer of 1944. It was during this summer that I was offered employment at the prestigious Tuskegee Institute in Tuskegee, Alabama.

When I think of my Tuskegee Institute years, 1944–1946, the stepping-stone image again comes to mind. Although, certainly, I did not accept employment at Tuskegee Institute with any desire to use the experience for my professional advancement there or elsewhere, I did respond positively to its offer simply because Tuskegee and I each needed and wanted what the other had.

Prior to making a final decision about employment at Tuskegee Institute, I felt it wise to obtain the advice of the Kansas City, Kansas

Selective Service Board and accept the job offer of Dr. Frederick D. Patterson, president of Tuskegee Institute.

Needless to say, I was relieved to have the opinion by the Selective Service Board. I immediately sent a telegram to Dr. Patterson, accepting the offer to be the director of band and orchestra at Tuskegee Institute. The offer became effective on September 1, 1944. Upon my arrival at Tuskegee Institute, I was assigned temporary housing at the Dorothy Hall Tuskegee guest-housing facilities.

I had an early orientation meeting with Dr. William L. Dawson, chairman of the Department of Music, Tuskegee Institute, during which I received the keys to the band hall building. The band building consisted of the following rooms: band rehearsal, band director's office, instrument storage, uniform storage, and equipment storage.

The marching and concert bands rehearsed five days each week during the fall and winter semesters. The orchestra rehearsed two times each week. The marching band presented pre-game and halftime shows at four or five home football games and at one or two off-campus football games, played in Columbus, Georgia, or in Montgomery or Birmingham, Alabama. The marching band varied in size from 72 to 108 members. The orchestra consisted of twenty to twenty-five members; the instrumentation consisted of violins, violas, violin-cellos, bass violins with supporting oboes, bassoons, B-flat clarinets, alto and tenor saxophones, trumpets, French horns, trombones, and tubas. The orchestra performed one selection at evening vespers, held on each Sunday. I arranged music in a way that enhanced the unusual instrumentation of the orchestra.

In addition, the marching band led the procession of students to Sunday morning church services from the dining hall to the Tuskegee Chapel. Since Tuskegee did not offer a major in music, student members in the bands and the orchestra had only minimal hope of improving their ability to perform on their instruments. Likewise, student instrumentalists had very little incentive to improve their musicianship, as scholarships or financial assistance was unavailable.

In addition, the music department did not offer any instrumental-music technical course to enhance students' musical growth and development. It did not take long for me to realize that the band and orchestra program at Tuskegee Institute had limited possibilities for enhancing the musical growth of its instrumentalists.

Florida A&M College
1887–1946

PRE-FOSTER YEARS

The authentic record book, *The History of Florida Agricultural and Mechanical University*, written in 1963 by Dr. Leedell W. Neyland and the late John W. Riley, indicates that since its inception, the Florida State Normal and Industrial College (the *original* name of the school later to become Florida A&M College) has expressed an interest in music. Thus, various musical groups, mostly of an impromptu nature, developed prior to 1892. However, Neyland and Riley reveal that since the only music teacher was also the full-time English instructor, the quality of the training was about what one would expect. Yet, I would think that accolades would have been in order for the lone-but-courageous English teacher who apparently knew that English, like music, was a universal language. For three years Mrs. Laura Clark provided music instruction. In addition, any teacher assigned a musical group automatically became a provider of music instruction. Despite the lack of instructors trained in music, college and student interest soared, and the number of musical organizations increased rapidly through the years.

Musical pursuits or endeavors took a significant upturn when Professor P.A. Von Weller, a musician of German descent, joined the college faculty as director of vocal and instrumental music in 1892. Reputed to have been trained in the Queen's Private Chapel, St. James, in London, Professor Von Weller proved to be a thorough teacher. Under Professor Von Weller's direction, students earned diplomas and certification through regular courses of study. In addition, through masses and oratories, his students were prepared for instrumental performances.

Further, college history indicates that for approximately two dollars per month (plus a twenty-five cent instrument-use fee) private music and organ lessons were available to students. During his tenure, 1892–1898, Professor Von Weller formed the first band at the college.

Again, an instructor of English provided services to music students. However, this time the teacher was also a music instructor: Mrs. Willia R. Harris. The interdisciplinary approach must have worked well because Mrs. Harris enjoyed the capable volunteer assistance of Professor C. H. Johnson who, in addition to having been trained in the natural sciences, was adept in music.

In 1910, the next band director was a talented volunteer, Professor Nathaniel Adderly. He provided extraordinary music services and organized the first marching and concert bands at the college. According to Neyland and Riley, during the first thirty years, a band existed only when students had their own instruments and only when instructors were available to assist the organization.

In 1918, the highly capable Herman Spearing of Jacksonville marched on the scene as bandleader. His band flourished through a variety of performances and activities, including chapel and open-air events, concerts, and military presentations. His group also played for special campus and sporting events. Spearing served until 1923.

In 1924, Arnold Lee, Sr. became band director. In efforts to build a permanent band, various alumni purchased and donated twenty instruments to the college and pledged continued donations. It was at that time when President J. R. E. Lee, Sr., petitioned the Board of Control to support the hiring of a bandleader who would organize a band and an orchestra that would enhance the welfare, training, and satisfaction of students. Realizing the need for innovative thinking as vital to the success of his request, President Lee prepared a job description that required the bandleader to serve in an assistant capacity in the Mechanical Arts Department. Professor Lee served until 1928.

As interest and pride in the band increased, so did donations. In 1927 the Honorable John L. Webb of Little Rock, Arkansas, gave the college $500 to erect a bandstand on the campus. His gift is said to have been the largest ever given by a colored donor. Appropriately, the "Webb Bandstand" was erected as a symbol of his support and generosity. Shortly thereafter, the college expressed its appreciation with a resolution:

> WHEREAS, The Honorable John L. Webb donated $500 to the Florida Agricultural and Mechanical College for the erection of this beautiful bandstand; and,
>
> WHEREAS, This bandstand has added beauty to our campus, spirit to our musical organization, inducements for others to join us, and, material value to our college;
>
> Be it Resolved, That the members of the band extend in this formal way a vote of thanks and deep appreciation to Honorable John L. Webb for this magnificent bandstand and for the fine spirit which prompted the gift.
>
> Be it further Resolved, that as we attempt to present concerts and keep harmony of musical tones, there shall be harmony in our organization in commemoration of the donor to whom we are profoundly indebted.

Subsequently, in 1928, the Board of Control was moved to approve funds for the band director position. Continuing the legacy of musical greatness among band directors was Captain W. Carey Thomas, hired in 1928, who became a legend in his own time. The list of his accomplishments in terms of various formations—all in one year (1928)—is impressive to say the least: a fifty-piece military and concert band, a twenty-five-piece symphony orchestra, a twenty-piece junior band, a fifteen-piece girls' orchestra, and a thirty-piece girls' drum and bugle corps. In 1929, the FAMC Military & Concert Band made two significant accomplishments. It performed at the South Florida Fair in Tampa and became the first Negro band whose performance was broadcast from Station WDAE. Professor Thomas served until 1930.

Captain W. Carey Thomas

Professor Leander Kirksey served as band director from 1930–1945. During those years, more college musical organizations received and accepted invitations to appear over the state and university station, WRUF at Gainesville. A graduate of Wiley College, Professor F. E. James served as director of the choral group. Subsequently, the band director and leaders of the various music groups earned respect throughout Florida and enjoyed many accolades. Afterward, the college musical groups received and honored numerous invitations.

By 1933 the band, glee club, choir, and other groups had covered the state with melodious music and goodwill. One hundred and two members strong in 1932, the college choir performed on major assembly programs. The symphonic orchestra performed at less important events. From Webb Bandstand on Sunday afternoons, the college band entertained legislators and other leaders. Also, the "Varsity Quartet" and the "FAMC Collegians" (a dance band) were popular. The dance band played for campus dances, which in themselves were ever-growing attractions among students.

Neyland and Riley's history of the college further indicates that added to band activities on campus were the regular Lyceum programs, which continued to culturally enrich the campus. Each year sponsors presented at least four nationally or internationally known artists.

Marian Anderson, Duke Ellington and his orchestra, Lionel Hampton, and José Greco's dance group delighted audiences, young and old alike. Symphonic groups and lecturers, such as Mordecai Johnson and W. E. B. DuBois, represented other artists who shared their talents with the campus community during the early years of band creation.

During the mid-30s, the choral phases of the music department developed at a commendable pace under the leadership of J. Harold Brown, who held the bachelor of music degree from Horner-Kansas City Conservatory and the master of arts degree from Indiana University. In addition to developing an outstanding college choir, which

FAMC Band 1946 Line of March

filled many engagements throughout the state, Brown trained the famous Florida A&M College Quartet, which performed at the Centennial Fair in Cleveland in 1936 and at the World's Fair in New York in 1939. In this respect, he followed in the footsteps of Norman L. Merrifield (M.S., Northwestern) and S. E. James (A.B., Wiley College), who had organized the "FAMC Quartet" in the early 1930s and had it perform at the World's Fair in Chicago, in 1933.

The College Band, under the direction of L. A. Kirksey, a graduate of Florida A&M College, endeavored to keep strides with the Division of Choral Music. However, with the outbreak of World War II, the sixteen-piece band, which played primarily for the traditional line of march, dwindled until it dissolved almost completely.

When I joined the music faculty in the summer of 1946 as band director, I was challenged to develop a band program that was, for all practical purposes, nonexistent.

Dr. William P. Foster
1946–1949

THE GRAY YEARS

O n the morning of June 1, 1946, my wife, Mary Ann, our two sons, our black cocker spaniel, Spekie, and I journeyed from Tuskegee, Alabama, to Tallahas-see, Florida, in an automobile owned and driven by our Tuskegee neighbor and friend, Dr. Alonzo Davis, dean, School of Education at Tuskegee Institute.

The scenario that preceded this trip took place at a football game between Florida A&M College and Tuskegee Institute at Crandon Stadium on the campus of Tuskegee Institute in October 1945. Among the fans and friends who observed the pregame and halftime performances by the Tuskegee Institute Marching Band under my direction were the president of FAMC, Dr. William H. Gray, Jr., and the Director of Student Affairs at FAMC, Mr. Moses G. Miles.

After the football game, I attended a meeting of Alpha Phi Alpha Fraternity. Two Alpha men in attendance were Dr. Gray and Mr. Miles. Following the meeting, I returned home for some much-needed relaxation. However, at about 11:00 or 11:30 p.m., Ann and I heard a knock at the door and were surprised by visitors in the persons of Dr. Gray and Mr. Miles.

After warm greetings, introductions, and get-acquainted overtures, our visitors complimented me on the performance of the Tuskegee Institute Marching Band and proceeded to state their mission. They wished to interest me in coming to Florida A&M College in Tallahassee, Florida, to develop a band that would "put FAMC on the map." In other words they wanted me to develop a band that would make Florida A&M College well known throughout the country. That night I was offered the position of band director at FAMC. I was interested.

I made a trip to Tallahassee, Florida, during the early spring of 1946 to have a meeting with Dr. Gray. The agenda of our meeting covered an in-depth discussion of expectations, needs, resources (or lack of resources), and challenges. Following a lengthy analysis of the job description, we agreed that I would establish an academic program for band and instrumental music that would meet the following requirements:

- Curricular structure for instrumental music B.S. degree

- Funding for new and additional courses

- Funding for basic additional faculty and staff

- Adequate budget for capital and expense requirements

- Establishment of a scholarship program to assist competent musicians to receive a college education in the areas of marching band, concert band, and ensembles

- Procurement of qualified and competent music faculty

- Adequate rehearsal, instruction, and classroom facilities

After a consensus on these items, President Gray and I addressed the last item on the agenda: compensation for the director. I agreed to accept employment at Florida A&M College, effective June 1, 1946.

Upon my arrival at FAMC, I was aware of the formidable task of starting with zero. My first task was to make a survey of equipment, instruments, and supplies. There was no band room. There were sixteen or seventeen broken instruments, of which three, perhaps four, were salvageable.

I came to FAMC with the under-standing that funds for musical schol-arships would be provided for band students. Mr. J. Harrison Thomas was chairman of the Department of Music at that time. The department consisted of six faculty members, fourteen music majors, and it offered the bachelor of science degree in music with majors in choral or instrumental music.

Lee Hall in the 1940s

The music department was housed in inadequate facilities located in Lee Hall. Faculty offices, studios, and classrooms were located on the third and fourth floors. Small rooms located on both sides of the auditorium stage were used for the band and choir. The concert band, the marching band, the men's and the women's glee clubs, and FAMC Collegian Jazz Band also used the Lee Hall auditorium stage for rehearsals.

Lee Hall was the only multistory brick building on campus used for instruction. The presence of a number of wooden buildings that were not in the best condition made Lee Hall look odd. The area looked more like an old military barracks than a college campus, such as the University of Kansas. I thought, "This is going to take some getting used to." Nevertheless, I was happy to be at FAMC and was looking forward to the challenge ahead.

FAMC Marching Band and Dr. Foster, in the center back row, 1947

Now, looking back on that period in our segregated history, especially in the southeastern United States, I suppose I should have been thankful that there was even a Lee Hall on the campus of FAMC. After all, the institution was a colored college campus. Back then, "separate but equal" was very separate and very unequal.

The Lee Hall auditorium was the only facility available for the presentation of concerts, recitals, programs, and assemblies. However, the Department of Music received some relief from its severe lack of space in 1947 and 1948. At that time, portable army barracks were set up at the rear of Lee Hall for classrooms, faculty offices and studios, band-instrument and band-uniform rooms, individual practice rooms, band-rehearsal rooms, and a music library.

Requisitions were processed for the purchase of new instruments, repair of the few instruments on hand, music and band accessories, office equipment, supplies, and miscellaneous merchandise. The department needed everything! When I generated the requisitions, I knew that funds were very limited. Therefore, I was happy to get whatever things the college could afford to provide the department.

Shortly after arriving at FAMC, I began to develop class schedules of applied-music offerings. I began planning shows for the marching band to perform at our football games. In addition, I contacted the placement offices of different colleges and universities and began to search for music faculty.

In my first year at FAMC, there was little time for relaxation. I had much work to do, and it was up to me to get it done. Besides encouraging the renovation of band facilities, completing requisitions for various things, contacting potential students and recruiting music staff, I had to secure a location for a band drill field.

Among the new students recruited were veterans returning after service in the armed forces. Veterans came from Tallahassee; nearby cities in Georgia; Norfolk, Virginia; Chicago, Illinois; Kansas City,

Kansas and Kansas City, Missouri; St. Louis, Missouri; and other locations that had high school bands.

With the opening of school in September 1946, I had organized my first band at FAMC with an impressive forty-five-member marching band. The counterpart of the 1946 marching band is the 1947 concert band.

The challenges I faced upon my arrival at Florida A&M College were monumental. The process and program of recruitment of prospective personnel was one of the first tasks. The recruitment program consisted of my identifying former band members, obtaining information regarding plans for the 1946 marching band of FAMC, and communicating with band directors in Florida, Georgia, Alabama, Kentucky, Virginia, Illinois, Missouri, North Carolina, South Carolina, and Louisiana.

FAMC Concert Band and Dr. Foster, in the center, on the Lee Hall stage, 1948

"Whew! What a tremendous job!" I often thought. "What have I gotten myself into?" I concluded, "Well, Pat, you're into it, now. No sense in despairing. You'll just have to make it work. Let's see what you're made of, really." I realized that, like the mother figure of Langston Hughes' famous poem, "The Negro Mother," I had to trudge on; there was no turning back for me. I realized, also, that in terms of emerging generations of band directors, I was the forerunner of the Black band director that was "not supposed to be." And the beat went on. It never stopped. "I must trudge on," I whispered to myself during my few quiet moments. Thanks, Langston.

The FAMU Band Motto

Can you imagine a band director who grew up in Kansas City, Kansas, having never before visited the southeastern United States relocating to Tallahassee, Florida, to become a teacher and an administrator?

Can you imagine the differences in culture, social etiquette, graces, and such that could exist between a colored teacher reared and educated in Kansas and colored students generally from the Panhandle of Florida in the 1940s and 1950s?

When I was just beginning to teach, to search for a successful career path, I was determined to develop an effective and successful band program at Florida A&M College in spite of the differences.

During the early years of my career, this country was legally segregated, especially in the "deep south." How was I going to get my music program off the ground? How was I going to teach my students all that I felt they needed to succeed? I was familiar with the legal expression, "Separate but equal education" and with the lifestyles inherent in the fabric of the United States of America. In the early years, "White was right" if you wanted to live. By that, I mean that if you were Black, Negro, or colored, you had to learn what was acceptable for Black and White people in order for you to be successful.

The best I could have expected when I arrived at FAMC was to have been given a chance to succeed. I tried to be as realistic about expectations as possible. I never forgot what my parents and grandparents and other supporters had taught me. My expectations had much to do with their expectations of me. They had always encouraged me to do my best, despite dismal circumstances. That's what I understood, and that was what I had in mind to do.

As I continued my work at FAMC, I realized that much of my success would depend on how my students responded to me. I would have to find a way to teach them and provide incentives that would result in a successful band program.

My students came from small farms, plantations, small country towns and inner-city cultures. They were all from the "deep south." Besides the need to find instruments, music books, and minimal dollars of financial support for students, I was faced with other concerns: What was I going to do about personal behavior? Social attitudes? Other such things?

After a year or so at FAMC, along with all the other preparations for a successful band program, I decided to create the band motto. I created the motto because I needed something to help me guide band students to a higher place, a level of excellence for which they were all striving. It gave them something by which they could live daily.

Band students and I were involved on a daily basis. I was interested in more than how well they played their instruments. I wanted to teach them about character, dress, self-discipline, personal etiquette, and other such things. The students needed daily reminders. They needed to be fine-tuned. In many cases their values needed some realignment.

The band motto was introduced to students during freshman orientation. From the very beginning of their introduction to the band program, the band motto became a part of their development. The motto was in all of our band publications. It appeared in the weekly schedules, on band-trip itineraries, and in the band handbook, which was also developed before 1950. My desire and plan were to have the motto perpetually before band members. I wanted it to become a part of their very being—their souls.

The following is the band motto developed for the Florida A&M University Band:

Highest Quality of Character, which encompasses the components of personal bearing, attire, and language.

Achievement in Academics, which is the purpose of students coming to the university in preparing for a career and life's work.

Attainment in Leadership, which should be exhibited by the organizational and operational structure of the band.

Perfection of Musicianship, which references tonal beauty, intonation, technique, articulation, and dynamic contrast phrasing.

Precision in Marching, which refers to point, drive, stationary position, knee lift, 30- 45- 60- and 90-degree knee lift, and instrument arc.

Dedication to Service, which is the basic function of the band to the university, the community, and its national and international publics.

Growing My Own Crop

Within two years and after the band had grown from forty-five to seventy-two members, I added the first dance steps to a band routine. It was the beginning of my concept of "band pageantry."

The "band pageantry" concept involves having all the creative ideas and thoughts coincide to give the music a "thematic thread." Included, also, must be a relevancy of selected music to the interests of the audience and the era. The rudiments and examples of my approach to "band pageantry" are presented in my instructional manual for band directors, *Band Pageantry: A Guide for the Marching Band*, published in 1968 by Hal Leonard Music, Inc., Winona, Minnesota.

We were always ready to try new things. Contrary to what you might have heard, however, not everything we tried worked. Yet, we kept experimenting and found that quite a lot of what we tried to do did work well most times. Our first dance steps were simple crossovers while band members moved their instruments either 30, 45, 90, or 180 degrees. The main features to that performance were the unison and the precision as the players executed those first movements to our theme song at the time: "Alexander's Ragtime Band."

On September 1, 1949, I replaced Mr. J. Harrison Thomas as chairman of the Department of Music at Florida A&M College. By 1950 the marching band consisted of 110 members and became widely known as the Marching "100" Band. It was about that time, also, that a "new sound" emerged that was said to describe the eighteen-piece percussion section, made up of four Scotch bass drums, four tenor drums, eight snare drums, and two pairs of cymbals.

During the early years, because of a very low budget, the dress attire for the FAMC Marching Band consisted of their personal dark-blue or black suits, trousers and coats; white shirts, black string ties; and black shoes—all furnished by the band members. The college purchased white web-cross belts, white spats, and black band caps. For several years after I arrived, the FAMC band donned blue and orange uniforms formerly used by the University of Florida marching band. However, orange and green were and still are the school colors at FAMU.

Another tremendous challenge I faced was the recruitment, evaluation, and training of initial faculty members. From 1946 to 1953, selections were made among selected band faculty and staff members from outstanding schools of music—institutions such as the University of Michigan, Ohio State University, the Julliard School of Music, and the Eastman School of Music.

Prior to and after recruitment, I evaluated faculty and staff as highly competent instructors and performers on their major instruments. Still, in some cases, I regretted to find that, despite outstanding musical qualifications, some employees did not measure up to my standards. In my estimation, or in terms of my standards, they lacked some of the values I felt our band members deserved and needed.

Some of the faculty and staff members could not relate to band students. They lacked the compassion and empathy needed in order for them to work effectively with our less musically endowed students. Also, they did not possess the necessary patience and genuine interest in students that was mandatory. Evident, too, was the fact that they lacked the required commitment, compassion, and dedication in their instruction and work.

I felt strongly (and still do) that successful and noteworthy educators must incorporate their full attention and compassion toward their students. I felt then, and feel now, that educators should realize that a strong key to a successful program includes conducting themselves with strong ethics, character, and respect in interaction with students. They must enhance the self-esteem of students, both individually and collectively. In fact, they must make students their first and foremost concern for care and nurturing. The expression, "I got mine; you get yours," was misleading and destructive to the type of program I was trying to build at FAMC.

Despite the circumstances and regardless of the problems, my staff and I had a job to do. I concluded that not only would we learn to be musical or band masters at FAMC but of our fate, too!

In recognizing our instructional dilemma, I decided that the situation required my developing and "growing" potential future faculty members who possessed the competence, performance, ability, commitment, dedication, compassion, interest, empathy, and desire needed. This was one of the best decisions I could have made during the formative years of the Florida A&M University Marching Band.

In my day, folks talked about "growing your own crop" to ensure that you got precisely what you needed—and in the right proportions. Thus, in terms of faculty members, my recruitment, evaluation, and training took on new purpose: the recruitment of what, today, FAMU terms "the brightest and the best." Also, the new method of recruiting staff would ensure that the brightest and the best brought more to the program than mere credentials and personal agendas. They had to exemplify wholesome values, a willingness to be constantly evaluated, and an acceptance and practice of exemplary training procedures.

My "growing your own crop" methods involved recruiting, evaluating, and training our own alumni, gleaned from our own fertile fields—or as today's students say, "the patch." (Incidentally, students coined the term "the patch" to describe the field on which the marching band practiced.)

The first music department and FAMU band alumni selected to join the faculty of the FAMU Music Department and band faculty staff was Leonard C. Bowie (fall of 1959).

In succession, several graduates from the FAMU Music Department and Instrumental Music Program were employed: Charles S. Bing (1960), Samuel A. Floyd and Ruffie Londen (1962), John H. Daniels, Jr. and Shaylor L. James (1965), Julian E. White (1973), Lindsey B. Sarjeant (1974), Wallace A. Clark (1997), and Shelby Chipman (1998).

Each of these faculty members met the qualifications and embraced the challenges. They worked cooperatively, diligently, compassionately, and productively. Realizing the need for advancement, each earned the master's and/or doctoral degree. Having a band faculty and staff of former band members moved our program forward successfully and enabled me to become successful as director of the Florida A&M University marching and symphonic bands, as well as an instructor for instrumental-music majors.

During my early years at Florida A&M College, little did I know that several decades later, the vow I took in the dean's office at the University of Kansas would come to full fruition. As I recognize this now, I humbly thank God and my many support groups for a dream come true—not only for my dream but more importantly for that of others.

Initially, there were some members of the armed forces in the band, about ten or twelve. There were only two females, and both of them were baton twirlers.

By 1947, I decided that we could develop a more functional band, one that would operate like a machine, and that if we had all males, we could drive. I didn't wish to impose that same requirement upon the young ladies. Thus, it was not until the passing of Title IV of the Civil Rights Act of 1975 that women were admitted into the band. Now, I am very pleased and delighted that the inclusion of females in the band finally happened. Today, one can't tell the females in the band from the males. The ladies have drive, musicianship, and marching qualities equal or superior to the males.

It is said that after arriving in Tallahassee in 1946, I astonished band members by throwing out everything they thought they knew. Well, I don't know about everything. I effected a number of discards in terms of instructional and marching techniques. Simply, I taught the band how to perfect double-time and triple-time or six steps per second movements. They learned to execute the "death cadence," an excruciatingly slow "one step every three seconds" exercise.

According to the late Nat Adderly, one of my first band students, later a jazz great, "Everything he (Foster) did was new; no one had ever seen anything like it, especially in terms of the precision. If the cadence was 120 beats or slower, the knee lift had to be 90 degrees. Something as simple as a right turn was broken into four steps."

Today, the "death march" requires great dexterity and poise. Each band member must look exactly like the drum major as the tempo goes down to thirty to forty steps and then back up to four to six times faster.

Basically, the success of the FAMU Marching Band results from a format of extensive variety and relevancy to the times. From the very beginning, we were an experimental band, which employed innovative and creative techniques, designs, and maneuvers. One of the band's keys to success is its penchant for organization, precision, high energy, and perfection. The band never reaches an apex of perfection, as we are always attempting to make improvements and refinements.

The evolutionary pageants staged by the FAMU Marching Band had a profound impact on the status of the "100." From the beginning of my tenure, the band has been an organization with the philosophy of trying out innovative maneuvers and techniques.

However, I believed in working, practicing, and re-practicing until we got everything just right. I've been said to work with a trumpet section for ten minutes just to clean up four notes. Further, someone has said that as a musical director, I pick up a melody and work with it like a fisherman meticulously unraveling a tangled line. It is also said that rather than skipping over rough spots, I focus on them. I admit those facts. I'm guilty.

However, those techniques work. I believe, notwithstanding the obvious flashiness of the band, that it is its superior musicianship that separates it from many other bands. We are known to play music, as well as march, dance, etc. We are first musicians and then marchers.

The first and foremost objective for band members is the development of sound musicianship. Training in sound musicianship is something that is accomplished through everyday experiences and, of course, practice. Musicianship encompasses competency in the beauty and quality of tone, intonation, execution of notes, and proper techniques, coupled with correct articulation.

Further, musicianship encompasses adherence to expression, phrasing, and interpretation, as well as knowledge of musical symbols, markings, signs, and terms. Musicianship encompasses sensitivity and understanding of style and form: listening while playing and, thus, recognizing and responding appropriately to melody, counter melody, filler, bass, harmonic, or ornamental parts. On the whole, good musicians must exhibit the ability to contribute effectively to the blend of the ensemble.

All of these traits assist in the awareness and an appreciation for fine music, whether band members are playing or listening, performing, or relaxing. Such an awareness and appreciation may be gained from the study of existing standard works and transcriptions for the band as well as from the great wealth of contemporary original works, which are being added to the literature yearly. An examination of the recognized composers who produce work for bands indicates that a wealth of fine literature has been written specifically for our medium.

In fact, a band's performance with a satisfactory or an exemplary degree of musicianship is directly related to the ability of the band director to teach the principles of basic musicianship and to motivate and inspire each student to develop positive attitudes toward superior performance. Correct instruction is essential in intonation (tuning and playing in tune), interpretation (adherence to and execution of elements of expression), tone production (quality, beauty, and projection), articulation (style of playing of notes within the phrase), technique (correct notes, note values, and rhythm), and ensemble blend and balance.

In terms of specifics, the format of our pregame and halftime shows are planned to not only entertain but also to encompass educational and cultural values. My hypothesis is that band shows can be educational as well as functional musical experiences if they are produced with a proper balance between accepted standards of music and of entertainment.

Our concept of the choreography is based upon the presentation of a total production consisting of (1) spectacular entrance with fanfare, (2) multi-drill-precision, circle patterns in motion-drill routines, (3) pageantry-picture formations with animation, (4) concert formation, and (5) dance routines. The music we select fits the movements of each segment of the show.

As I worked with band members and my faculty and staff, I valued relevance as a key element to acceptable performances. Some of my former students have said that I sought to produce shows based on actual human personalities and events, not on military music written a hundred years earlier. I accept that assessment; my imagination seemed to have been working at full speed on a daily basis. This was apparent in the introduction of dance steps intertwined with what has been called "the best of contemporary music: jazz, rock—whatever got people off their seats." We became known for unusual formations, humorous depictions, etc.

It has been said that many of my "wildest routines," the ones that were said to jerk entire stadiums to their feet and halt football games and turn parades into street parties, generally came to me in the quiet moments of dawn. It's true. I must admit that sometimes in the quiet moments of dawn, I do see formations, steps, etc., with clarity: band members stepping, strutting, twisting, snaking—horns high, trombones low, drum major leaping, turning, landing in a split.

It has been said that our band is always full of surprise audience-pleasing techniques—that when it advances toward and/or steps on the field in synchronized fashion, it slides, glides, slithers, swivels, rotates, shakes, rocks, and rolls. It leaps to the sky, does triple twists, and drops to the earth without a flaw—without missing either a beat or a step. In addition, it is said that with all units moving in rapid but precise formation, fans are hard-pressed to keep up with the extraor-dinary panoramic or kaleidoscopic view of the now three-hundred-plus band members, all doing their collective but individual thing! Is that a musical paradox, or what?

Among the various dance performances are some favorites: the old Mashed Potato, the Charleston, the Snake, the California Worm, and the Tootsie Roll.

In summation, our band pageants have great current and legendary appeal because they fascinate the eyes and ears of the spectators. In other words, our band pageants relate to the audience.

It may surprise you to know that because of the recognition of the FAMU band in the mid-50s: my doctoral dissertation, written in 1955, was accepted with no references. It was most unusual that professors would permit anything like that, but they did. The band's reputation allowed the committee to view my dissertation as original and authoritative. Thirteen years later it was published under the title *Band Pageantry*, and it has been the bible for marching-band directors for thirty or more years. One unusual thing about that book is that it is just as fresh and pertinent today as it was in 1968 when it was published—because it deals with fundamentals.

Dr. William P. Foster
1950–1962

THE GORE YEARS

The George W. Gore years at FAMC were filled with hard work, trial and error, and increased growth for the Department of Music and the band program at FAMC. The school's motto during the Gore years was "Quality Is FAMC's Measure." As president of FAMC, Dr. Gore urged all members of the college to exemplify the motto in their daily campus interaction. In addition, administrators, faculty, staff, and students were encouraged to spread the good news that FAMC was the quality college to attend—the place to be. Students were thoughtfully and thoroughly taught so that they would be well prepared for productive lives in their respective communities. Administrators and teachers alike kept close vigil on students' progress and stages of development as a means of ensuring society a finished and quality product at graduation.

President Gore fostered and illustrated ethical behavior, sound judgment, academic superiority, personal confidence, visionary planning, cooperative efforts, and positive thinking. He worked tirelessly to foster cultural, religious, social, and civic activities among the college and the Tallahassee communities. It was not uncommon for students and community non-students to find themselves the honored guests in the home of President Gore and Mrs. Gore on Sunday afternoons. Their campus home, warmly referred to by the Gores and students as "Sunshine Manor," was truly symbolic of its name.

The president never wavered in his belief in the tremendous potential of the college. At every opportunity, he advocated that FAMC seek and foster quality above all else. According to Neyland and Riley, this stance was reiterated in President Gore's 1950 assembly address: "We propose to lead. We propose to set the proper examples ... build a school that stands for friendliness, quality, and leadership."

As people began to buy into Dr. Gore's philosophy and to support his efforts, the college began to flourish. At that time, so did the activities and performances of the marching band. We marched in the twenty-nine-year-old Festival of States' Annual Parade and became the first Negro band to participate. We were humble and proud. These performances were the forerunners of other wonderful firsts for the marching band. We continued to perform as unofficial recruiters; students and their parents viewed our performances as positive indicators of their future success at the college. By the mid-50s, the marching band enjoyed national recognition, and we took pride in offering both entertainment and service. We were beginning to become a FAMC and Florida treasure.

Perhaps in Cecil Murray's tribute to President Gore on the occasion of his inauguration, the course was charted for the marching band and for all other college organizations and entities. Specifics of the tribute are worthy of note:

For this glorious institution is our home, and you, its president, are father to hundreds of sons and daughters. Now, father, this is our pleasure: we want an FAMC of which all the world can be proud. We want a university with open doors. We want a haven of peace, void of internal strife, and resounding with the spirit of brotherhood. We want a faculty conscious of student needs—carefully selected, duly recognized, amply rewarded, and reasonably secure. We want a student body ever aware of our shining ideals.

Thus when the choir sings "A Balm in Gilead," when the band plays the "Victory March," when athletes reach their peak in performance, when scholars seek to outdo themselves; when FAMCeans all over the world feel the heart, the head, the hand, and the field; when the glorious dreams of a past generation become the staunch realities of this school today—then will you know that your sons and daughters love you, honor you, and thank you... and, for us, that time is now.

May the ship of affairs find a peaceful harbor in you, sir. May the depression of spirit that comes with tormented age never be felt by you. May your hands never tremble and your eyes never dim. May you live to take the immortal levy undaunted. God be with you, Sir. We're with you all of the way.

Indeed, one could say that victory has been a band theme song that has never ended, a refrain that lingers in the recesses of the mind, despite setbacks and challenges. From the Gore years of the 50s throughout his tenure, member interest and participation in the band increased monumentally, as did accomplishments. (Undoubtedly, band members and their teachers are to be commended.)

During the Gore administration, the marching band grew from 110 to 132 members. The band incorporated a dance routine using the music of "Alexander's Ragtime Band" in its halftime show at the Orange Blossom Classic in Miami, Florida, in 1952.

In 1962, with the assistance of Dr. Beverly Barber, professor and director of dance at the university, dance became a regular part of the band's halftime shows.

Meanwhile, President Gore was relentless in his desire and efforts to move FAMC to the level of "university," and indeed, with the constant urging and efforts of President Gore, the Board of Control, and various leaders and support groups, Florida Agricultural and Mechanical College (FAMC) became Florida Agricultural and Mechanical University (FAMU) in 1953. Prior to this success, however, the Division of Graduate Studies had already awarded 124 master's degrees. Fred Scott, a teacher at Howard Academy in Monticello, Florida, was the first to earn the master of education degree.

From 1953–1960, 797 master's degrees were conferred. After the college gained university status, Mrs. Gore, the "first lady" received the first master of science degree awarded at FAMU. Why was no one surprised to learn that Mrs. Gore's thesis was entitled "A Study of Scholastically Superior Students in Sixty Negro Colleges and Universities"?

Clearly, both the earlier and the latter Gore years were good ones for the university family and for the Marching "100." Undeniably, the Gore era represented a time of abundant growth for the university and a time of maturation for the marching band.

Since Florida A&M College became Florida A&M University, of course, our band name also changed to the "Florida A&M University Marching Band." You can't imagine how proud—no—how ecstatic we were when the first complete set of uniforms for the band was purchased in 1956 from Ostwald Uniform Company, Staten Island, New York! Brand new, beautiful FAMU uniforms! The right name and the right colors! In grand celebration, we began playing more enthusiastically, stepping higher, marching faster, and voicing our pleasure "louder and prouder" than ever. In short, that's when we began our characteristic high-energy ways of playing and marching that would ultimately take us to Paris, France, thirty-nine years later.

The FAMU Band Camp

The FAMU Band Camp is the result of a concept that I developed in the early 1950s. After several years of contemplation and brainstorming ideas with the other members of my staff, I devised a program to meet the following needs:

- Bring about an increase in recruitment of talented and competent instrumentalists;

- Bring about an increase in the size of the FAMU Marching Band; and

- Bring about an increase in majors in the Department of Music.

I developed a booklet to serve as a guide and source of information on the structure and preparation of a summer band camp to embrace grade levels seven through twelve.

The booklet explained that instruction would include the following offerings:

- The marching band

- The symphonic band

- The concert band

- Ensembles to include brass winds, woodwinds, percussions, octet, sextet, quintet, quartet, and trio

The booklet explains the use of a support system that included personnel such as conductors, staff members, student assistants, office staff, secretaries, and clerks. Information on how to provide room and board for band camp participants, the schedule of events, and use of facilities were included in the band-camp guidelines.

Also included in the guidelines were the following: information on program operations, performances, awards, scholarships, a financial aid program, an auxiliary program for majorettes, flags, rifles, drum majors, outstanding performance, achievement awards, best sections, playing, and marching and dancing overall.

Communication forms, form letters, selections of music, social activities, camp attire, daily concert, health-consent forms, personal-information forms, health forms, medical forms, and transportation-committee information were provided in the guidelines.

Band-camp rules; policies; regulations; a checklist for campers; and financial schedules for boarding and for day campers, chaperones, monitors, facilities coordinator, and staff, etc. were also included in the guidelines.

The guidelines booklet identified student responsibilities. Each student would be responsible for bringing his or her instrument, folding portable music stand, pillows, camp drum major or majorette uniforms, and other essentials. A checklist was developed to assure compliance.

There were a number of good outcomes that could be realized from a FAMU Marching Band Camp. Besides the fact that the camp would help the university in its recruitment efforts, the camp would also give prospective band students the opportunity of learning and actually performing basic techniques of playing, marching, and other things associated with improving the proficiency on marching and playing. All movements are extensions of basic drill fundamentals.

The camp would give my staff the opportunity early on to identify excellent or potentially quality students, who could be encouraged to attend FAMU and participate in the marching band. In turn, the students who attended the camp would return to their schools and share what they had learned. This could improve the quality of their individual bands and inform others of the Marching "100."

The camp would be beneficial to band staff and student leaders. The staff would be involved in teaching the concepts of basic musicianship including quality of sound, phrasing, articulation and accent, and the concept of the singing tone. The staff would be able to teach the basic elements of marching-band techniques—all the basic concepts that pertain to the movements of the body as they relate to marching-band techniques. Movements of the body included understanding the use of the foot, the leg, the knee, the hand, the head, and so on. Generally, the students would learn to think in 30, 45, 60, 90, 180 degrees.

My staff would teach the crucial aspect of learning the routines. Individual students would be taught a routine by doing repetitive movements. Movements involved motor skills which, to perfect the movement, require repetition. The development of precision requires the execution of stationary positions. The eye interprets movement based on learned stationary positions. The basic drill is important because all other movements are created on the drill of the bandsman. The concepts are thoroughly explained in my book, *Band Pageantry*.

Although the band camp concept began in the early 1950s, we were unable to conduct the program at FAMU due to budgetary constraints. In 1990, more than thirty-seven years after developing the band camp concept, the Department of Music received the financial backing of continuing education. That was the first year of a very successful summer band camp program.

1998 FAMU Band Camp participants

A couple of years before our first band camp, I gave all of my conceptual data and my printed band-operations manual concerning band camp implementation to Dr. Julian White for his review and implementation. Dr. White was given charge of the band-camp project and was appointed director of the Florida A&M University Summer band camp. I was assistant director. The director of the band camp needed to be someone with the time for preparation, planning, and execution of all tasks involved. Dr. White was the right person for the job and has been an excellent administrator of the summer band camp.

Dr. William P. Foster
1963–1979

NATIONAL TV DEBUT

B y 1963 the Marching "100" had been the recipient of numerous recognitions. However, what happened in 1963 was considered by band staff and supporters to be the icing-on-the-cake award.

In 1963 the band made its first national television debut at the Pro-Bowl Football Game, which was televised by CBS from the Orange Bowl Stadium in Miami, Florida. That initial national television appearance seemed to have set the stage, or opened the door, for many similar appearances.

Some of the band's national television performances include the following: 1964, Pro-Bowl Football Game; 1964, NFL Championship Game; 1968, AFL All-Star Game on NBC; 1969, AFL All-Star Game; 1969, NFL game between the Boston Patriots and the Miami Dolphins; 1975, NFL game between the Philadelphia Eagles and the Washington Redskins; 1981, *60 Minutes* documentary on CBS; 1983, ABC News *20/20*; 1983, US Information Agency TV Satellite File for World-Wide Coverage; 1986, Fifteenth Anniversary of Walt Disney World National Television Special, ABC-TV; 1989, French Government's selection as the official US representative at the Bicentennial Celebration of the French Revolution, i.e., Bastille Day, in Paris, France (worldwide coverage); 1993 and 1997, State of Florida's representative to march in President Clinton's Inaugural Parade.

A SPECIAL LETTER

The FAMU Marching "100" Band was featured on ABC's *20/20* news magazine program in 1983. The taping crews from the network were in Tallahassee two weeks before the show aired to film the band's pre-season freshman drills. The following letter, dated August 23, 1983, was received from Jeffrey A. Panzer, producer of ABC News *20/20*, and Stephanie Cassell, associate producer of ABC News *20/20*:

> Dear Dr. Foster, Dr. White, the entire staff and band members of FAMU:
>
> It is highly unusual in the roller-coaster world of television broadcasting that a relationship between a production crew and the individuals they are doing stories with cultivate into a strong feeling of sincerity, compassion, respect, and most importantly, love. This special type of relationship I feel fortunate enough to have shared with all of you.
>
> As I mentioned to the entire band the evening before Stephanie and I departed to New York, my background is one that deals mostly with superstar profiles of entertainers in the music business. After spending nine days in Tallahassee, the realization struck me that every single one of you are the real superstars, not just in the field of music but also in life itself.
>
> You showed me the meaning of dedication and motivation for which you should all be commended. I honestly hope that the forty million American viewers on Thursday night can capture at least one quarter of

what you have given me. If they do, I believe we will all be winners!

Again, thank you for everything; and long after

this piece is finished, I will still be practicing my "One, Two, Three, and Four" forever.

With much respect and admiration,
Jeffrey A. Panzer and Stephanie Cassell
ABC News *20/20*

The letter from the ABC News *20/20* producers meant so much to all of us associated with the FAMU Department of Music and Marching "100" Band. We were encouraged by it. Our future looked good, and we were able and willing to do what was necessary to continue our march to glory.

Although the band received national recognition in the 60s, those were years of turmoil and change for Americans. The attitudes that were present in the general community were reflected in what was happening at Florida A&M University.

University president Gore wanted everyone to focus on excellence (striving to become the best that we could be); however, some members of the FAMU family saw him as a Black man who was doing everything he could to keep Black people in their places. They felt that he didn't want us to rock the boat. Instead, he wanted us to be submissive, accept what others determined to be our roles in life, and focus on areas of development that were opened to Blacks. While Dr. Gore was trying to show the world how "good" FAMUans could be, a storm—a great human movement—was underway, one to which even the protected walls of FAMU would have to give way.

When John Fitzgerald Kennedy became our national president in 1961, it was as if God had sent us a White man to deliver us from the suppression of White rule, dominance, and punishment. Every time President Kennedy spoke, we listened. We knew that he could make a difference in our lives in this country. We did not know how much of a difference, but with him in office, Black people had hope.

While we held high the Kennedy banner, we were also encouraged by the work of Dr. Martin Luther King, Jr. and the Southern Christian Leadership Conference (SCLC). We were encouraged by the work of the National Association for the Advancement of Colored People (NAACP), the Congress of Racial Equality (CORE), and the other organizations. We needed all of them. As they raised issues, local civil rights leaders from our community churches stepped forward. We were hopeful of a better day for us. We were tired of the conditions in which we had to live just because of the color of our skin. We were hopeful that change was going to come, and we needed it.

A forerunner of the desired change was the FAMU Marching "100" Band. By the early 1960s, the Marching "100" Band was getting some recognition within the Black community and throughout the nation. There were schools like the University of Michigan that knew about the Marching "100" Band and acknowledged its contributions.

However, the Marching "100" Band was a "Negro band." To many of our White neighbors, that meant that we had better know our place and stay in it. We at FAMU had something great that we wanted to show the world during the early 1960s, but with the social upheaval that was taking place around us, basically, the Marching "100" Band—outside the Black community—was just another "Negro band." There was much we wanted to do at FAMU, but we were limited by the restraints put on us by controlling forces in the United States of America.

The Honorable John Fitzgerald Kennedy, president of the United States of America, was assassinated On November 22, 1963. When I heard the news, I did not know what to do or what to say. I was in shock. I thought, "My God, they have killed the president. What are we going to do?" The FAMU family really did not know what to do. We grieved right along with others who loved President Kennedy. We had had such great hopes that he would make a change for the better in the country. We had been behind him, 100 percent. Now he had been killed. "Oh, my God! What will happen now?" I wondered.

When President Kennedy was killed, the football season was nearing an end. Yet, the Marching "100" Band had two more performances to give at FAMU football games: a home game and our own Orange Blossom Classic in the Orange Bowl in Miami, Florida. Our pregame performances for both games were devoted to the memory of our fallen leader, President John F. Kennedy. During that troubled time, band members, my staff, and I did the best that we could to express our deepest sympathy to the family of our fallen president by remembering him in our performances. This period in the history of the FAMU Marching Band was difficult, especially for the students. They had had such great expectations. Now they would have to cope with more difficult times ahead.

In 1963, President Lyndon Baines Johnson, who became president after the assassination of President Kennedy, led efforts to enact civil rights legislation in this country. President Kennedy's death was not in vain. Good did come from it, although it would have been more satisfying had he lived to see the civil rights legislation enacted. In 1964, the United States Congress passed the Civil Rights Act.

As the 1960s evolved, there were struggles for civil rights everywhere in the United States. Florida was not ignored. FAMU students marched and sat-in just like all the other supporters of equal rights in this country. Regardless of the difficult situation, we heard from everyplace in this country that "We are not going to be turned around."

By 1968, the FAMU Marching "100" Band was electrifying audiences with its high-stepping, fast-marching, and spirited dancing routines. "The Hundred" played its music in a way that made the audience stand up and take notice. Some people thought that there was no way for the FAMU band to get any better. We had made a name for ourselves, and we were moving forward, marching to a beat that could only emanate from the "Hill" (FAMU).

Dr. Martin Luther King, Jr., began his work in civil rights in the mid-1950s. In 1964, he received the 1964 Nobel Peace Prize. He spoke for me. He marched for me. In the end he gave his life for me. How valuable was he to you and me? It's as if God sent him to us to do what he did. Just as our prior hope was in President Kennedy, so it was in Dr.

King. He was brave. He had iron courage. Most importantly, he cared about you and me!

Shockingly and unfortunately, on April 4, 1968, Dr. Martin Luther King, Jr. was shot and killed in Memphis, Tennessee. It was obvious to me during this time that some people hated the idea of freedom, equality, and fairness for everyone. Moreover, they were willing to kill to assure the continuation of their way of life.

The death of Dr. King devastated our community. The children of our community, some of them at FAMU, rose up in anger to avenge their fallen leader. Not only did Blacks feel the pain of Dr. King's death but so did morally decent Whites and other non-Blacks who would not, or could not, look the other way any longer.

When good people of all races stood together for justice, Florida A&M University and its family of supporters stood tall with others to make a difference in this country. I wanted the "Hundred" to be a part of that difference. I wanted my staff to work even harder. I wanted our performances to be even better than they had been.

The FAMU Band Sound

I n the midst of the social and political turmoil of the 1950s and
1960s, I continued my search for the music that was playing
in my mind.

As I mentioned earlier in this book, I began "growing my own
crop" of potential faculty members before 1950. I was developing a
group of people who, I hoped, could help me produce the sounds of
music that continued to play in my head. I wanted so very much to
hear the sounds in my head actually played by musicians. I wanted
to conduct a group of outstanding young musicians at FAMU as they
played the sounds I had heard since my high school days in Kansas
City, Kansas.

I mentioned "growing my own crop" of potential faculty members
because a select few of my music students did become my eyes and ears,
my hands and feet, and my arms and legs. They became my everything as we and other outstanding faculty and staff continued in search
of the "Foster Sound," referred to today as the "FAMU Band Sound."
My initial tonal band concept came from the symphony orchestra. I
was impressed with the artistry and refined sound of the symphony
orchestra. It made a lasting impression upon me. Therefore, I was

interested in having the FAMU band sound like an orchestra with respect to a refined and beautiful sound. I wanted the band to have a beautiful ensemble sound.

The concept of the FAMU band sound had its beginning during my experience as student director of the Sumner High School Band and Orchestra. The image imprinted during my junior and senior high school experience while I played the violoncello was profound. This energized and singing tonal perception was personified and confirmed during my music education from 1941 through 1943. During that time, Mr. Edwin W. Peters tutored me on the basic elements of musicianship in performance in Springfield, Missouri.

My image of sound has the elements of movement and beauty, regardless of the articulation and tempo. The enhancement of every note played results in a sound of beauty. This sound quality is magnified as homogeneous and heterogeneous instruments are added to the ensemble. The texture of the ensemble sound is enriched and enhanced by each added component of sound to the chord structure.

Other musicianship components include articulation, the melody, the countermelody, the bass line, the harmonic filler and rhythm patterns, dynamic contrast, phrasing, and other factors such as ensemble blend and balance, tempo, etc.

One of the essential items in the development of the FAMU band sound is correct tuning of ever y instrument in the band. Creating a well-tuned band is the first and the most important step in the development of the FAMU band sound.

Without the band being tuned to an almost perfect degree, the development of the FAMU band sound is impossible. A band that is not tuned will emit a clash of sounds, which will make it impossible for that band to obtain a beautiful band sound.

The FAMU band sound is beautiful and alive. It is moving and energized. The perception of tone and timbre produced by each band member has its imagery conceived and imbedded in my ear and transmitted via osmosis to each member of the band being conducted. I analyze the sound that is produced by the band. I listen for the ringing overtone series property of each tone produced so that the final product is a sound of sonority—a sound that sings. This process requires absolute concentration. It requires accurate timing of each instrument. All other properties of musicianship, including expression techniques of crescendo, decrescendo, array of accents, cadre of articulation techniques, phrasing, and tempos are included in the creation, or development, of the particular sound that is being sought. This is a state-of-mind happening. The final phase in the process involves cohesion and routine.

I remember the first concert band that I had at FAMC. It originated in the spring of 1947. At that time, I attempted to have the band emit a fine sound with clarity and beauty—a refined sound. During the 1940s, generally speaking, band performances had been kind of loud and rough. In contrast, I wanted to have a refined sound, the type of sound that I heard in a recording of a Felix Mendelssohn composition. The orchestra had a sound that I liked. I wanted the FAMU band to have a sound like that.

When I talk about "Instruction on Performance" I am talking about how I wanted a piece to sound. In 1947, much of what I had to relate to was based on the symphonic orchestra—the refinement of music. I loved the sound that emitted from a finely tuned band.

During that time, I did little if any rearranging of the pieces we played. The compositions were purchased and played as they were written. However, I would review and add numerous musical marks and notations of my own, which would result in the piece being played in the way I conceived it. In a way, I suppose, I was beginning to teach my students the "Foster Sound," or what is universally referred to today as the "FAMU Band Sound."

Students in the FAMC band in the late 1940s were not always prepared to read the music placed before them. The type of sound I wanted from the FAMC band was in my mind. I heard it all the time. There was just one problem: how to get my students to play the sound that I wanted the world to hear. Although I would write in markings that represented how I wanted the music played, the students in the band at that time were not musically gifted enough to understand my markings. It did not take me long to realize that until I had better-prepared students, in addition to writing in markings, I would also have to sing or hum to the students the way I wanted the piece played. I don't know if the first few years of students in the band ever learned what my markings meant.

Eventually, our students became better prepared for what we had to offer. They more easily understood and were able to follow the musical notations that I wrote in on musical pieces. The "FAMU Band Sound" was improving.

The trumpet fanfares that we love had their origin in the late 1940s with my first music staff. Much of the time, we made up tones, or some derivative of them, and eventually refined them into what we wanted to hear at FAMC. Once we began to develop these unique sounds, they just became a part of the FAMC band culture.

The drum cadences that we love so much today also began in the late 1940s. Mr. Robert Elliot, a graduate of the School of Music, University of Michigan at Ann Harbor, was the first instructor of percussion at FAMC. He was an outstanding percussionist. His work was instrumental in the creation of the cadence identified with the "FAMU Band Sound." Later, Mr. James Latimer, a graduate of Indiana University, was added to my teaching staff. He established our first percussion ensemble.

In the 1940s and 1950s I believed that the best marching band program in the country was at the University of Michigan where Dr. William D. Revelli was director of bands. The first place from which I recruited instructors was the placement office of the University of Michigan. Dr. Revelli and I continued our relationship into the '90s.

Early in my career at FAMC, I enjoyed listening to a number of records produced by the University of Michigan School of Music. Although I had already begun to write in musical markings to suggest how I wanted FAMC band music to sound, as of 1950, I had not begun to *arrange* the music we played. However, that soon changed.

The records produced by the University of Michigan fascinated me. The University of Michigan band could take the simplest of songs and turn them into musical wonders. I was very excited about what I was hearing. Nevertheless, my understanding of musical theory was focused on applied-music theory. Still, I wanted to know about the music that was being played by students at the University of Michigan band.

During that time, the music arranger for the University of Michigan School of Music was Mr. Jerry Bilik. I wanted to know more about what he was doing. To this end, I invited him to come to FAMC and conduct a workshop on marching band arranging for my staff and me. He accepted my invitation. I cannot begin to explain to you how happy I was that such an outstanding arranger was coming to Florida A&M College to help us understand what he was doing. I could hardly wait for him to arrive.

Mr. Bilik was very helpful to our program. During his workshop, I began to notice that his arrangements included an innovative bass line and a counter melody that complimented the melody with an independent line. The way the bass line, melody, and countermelody worked together was most innovative. The most important part was the melody line of the trumpets, cornets, and clarinets.

With the techniques of Mr. Jerry Bilik, I found that I could strengthen any line so that it could be clearly heard. It became clear to me that Mr. Bilik was an expert in applied-music theory. However, he was not satisfied to remain captured within defined rules governing the relationship among bass line, melody, and countermelody theory.

Truly, Mr. Bilik was an explorer, a researcher, and a creative genius who had wanted to go beyond the simple to the more complex and had done so. He had made the jump successfully. Once I understood  what he was doing, I was ready to follow him to new dimensions in music development and appreciation. In fact, I was prepared to jump even higher than he had. I decided then and there that the FAMC band program was ready to go where no band had ever gone before.

Perhaps Mr. Jerry Bilik did not realize at the time the support he had given to our program. He was gracious. Not only did he teach us what we needed at the time, but he did not charge us for his services. We only paid for his travel and room and board. Mr. Bilik told me that it was an honor for him to be asked to come to Florida A&M College. We will always be indebted to Mr. Jerry Bilik and the director of bands at the University of Michigan, Dr. William D. Revelli. With the knowledge gained from the workshop, my staff and I began to arrange our music to suit our taste.

I felt that our pregame and halftime programs should be more than what was expected; I thought they should be shows that were contemporary, spirited, and satisfying to our audience. We sought to outplay, outmarch, and outdance all other bands. We did not want to imitate but to be imitated. We wanted all people, especially Black folks, to really enjoy what we were doing. We wanted to develop a world-renowned marching band at Florida A&M College.

The "FAMU Band Sound" was fully established once Mr. Lindsey Sarjeant was added to my teaching staff in 1974. Mr. Sarjeant is the music arranger for the FAMU Department of Music. His creative ability to arrange was the missing link in the FAMU band sound. Once he was in place at FAMU, the sound was complete. The sound that I had been trying to produce since my years in the Sumner High School Marching Band and Orchestra was now a reality.

The FAMU Marching Band, which grew to 329 musicians by 1995, was appreciative and proud of each opportunity to serve the people of the state of Florida, the nation, and the world via national and international television appearances. Sometimes, fans ask what is it about our band that makes it popular with or sought after by television networks. One response I offer is that marching bands must have and demonstrate a unique ability to fully and continually engage the eyes and ears of the television audience.

Thankfully, our Maker has fashioned the FAMU Marching Band to do just that, not as a matter of superficial response to a request but as a matter of course. What we do and what you see and hear equate to who we are. It's routine, it's natural, and it's genuine. With our band, as Flip Wilson used to say, "What you see is what you get."

In addition, bands have to be innovative, spirited, and talented. They must be able to play music, not make noise. They must be able to march—and in our case—to sing and dance. They must be creators, not imitators. They must be leaders, not followers. They must be originals. In addition, presentations must have focus; they must not lose their direction or abort their purpose. They must consider relevancy to the times and establish empathy with the audience. Finally, they must not make the mistake of being like dangling participles by functioning without a clear mission in their presentations. They must pay close attention to being able to entertain and educate their audiences.

Dr. William P. Foster
1980–1989

THE MCDONALD'S ALL-AMERICAN
HIGH SCHOOL BAND

O ne of the high points of my career was serving as director of the McDonald's All-American High School Band. My role as director of this prestigious musical organization was a catalyst for my professional career. During my directorship of the McDonald's All-American High School Band from September 1980 through November 1991, some people began to feel that I had become what they termed a "national celebrity." Thus, I was accorded titles such as *one* of the greatest band directors and the country's *greatest* band director.

From 1980 through 1991, I conducted the McDonald's All-American High School Band in several selections from the ice rink of Rockefeller Center in New York on the *Today Show*. I appeared in interviews with Willard Scott in two impromptu set conversations. This was national television coverage of the first magnitude.

For ten years, 1980 through 1991, the McDonald's All-American High School Band made several significant performances:

- in the Macy's Day Parade on Thanksgiving Day in New York City;
- in the Tournament of Roses Parade in Pasadena, California;
- in the Fiesta Bowl Parade with national television exposure in Phoenix, Arizona; and
- in the Children's Parade on national television in Chicago, Illinois.

In addition, the McDonald's All-American High School Band presented annual concerts at various places:

- Carnegie Hall, with nationally known artists
- Town Hall in New York City
- Orchestra Hall in Chicago, Illinois

Plus, the McDonald's All-American High School Band presented one-time concert performances at these places and events:

- Jordan Hall, New England Conservatory of Music
- Music Educators National Conference at the Kennedy Center in Washington, D.C., and Brooklyn Academy of Music, New York City.

The McDonald's Corporation officers, directors, and staff associates were great people with whom to work during the New York and California events. The GolinHarris Public Relations Agency managed and supervised all operations for the McDonald's Band. It made all arrangements for band operations, including transportation, room and board, special outings, and schedules of activities. Transportation and room and board accommodations were first class.

The public relations agency was responsible for producing video and audiocassettes of the McDonald's Band in the Macy's Thanksgiving Day Parade. It was responsible for setting up my interview at Rockefeller Center with the NBC *Today Show*. It handled the Central Park Press Day and concerts at Carnegie Hall and Town Hall. Arrangements were made for me to attend Broadway shows, go on New York tours, and enjoy special breakfast and dinner meals at the World Trade Center and Mama Leone's.

I remember the annual Thanksgiving dinners that were arranged for those of us who were associated with the McDonald's All-American High School Band. The dinner was highlighted with a whole turkey on each table. There were eight place settings on all tables. The dinner was a grand occasion for everyone involved.

As director of the band, I had complete responsibility and authority for the selection of band members and the music to be played for every event. I was also responsible for selecting the band staff personnel.

During my stay as band director of the McDonald's All-American High School Band, Dr. Julian E. White was my drillmaster and director of piccolos, B-flat clarinets, and saxophones. Mr. Lindsey B. Sarjeant was band arranger and director of trumpets and horns. Mr. Charles S. Bing was director of trombones, baritone horns, and tubas. Mr. Jay Wannamaker was director of percussion. The band staff personnel were an outstanding group of musicians, teachers, and administrators.

Beautiful red sweaters with McDonald's All-American High School Band emblems affixed were furnished to the band personnel including the band staff.

The New York trip revolved around the Macy's Thanksgiving Day Parade. The students and staff arrived in New York seven days before Thanksgiving and departed for their homes on Thanksgiving afternoon. The California trip was centered around the Tournament of Roses Parade on New Year's Day. The band personnel arrived in Los Angeles on December 26th, the day after Christmas. The band departed on the afternoon of January 1st, New Year's Day.

The Band was transported by air from Los Angeles to Phoenix, Arizona, on December 28th to march in the Fiesta Bowl Parade. Upon return from Phoenix to Los Angeles, the Band put on a fifteen-minute performance at the civic center for the McDonald's Corporate Dinner. The corporate officers and board members were in attendance at this event. The attendance was estimated at three hundred to four hundred people. During our travels, we never lost a band member.

These events were duplicated each year in New York and in California from 1980 to 1989.

The apex of my career as a band director was my experience as director of the McDonald's All-American High School Band. I have compiled a book of letters received from members of the McDonald's Band. These letters are testimonies of their experiences as members of the Band.

The Sudler Intercollegiate Marching Band Trophy

T hroughout my years of service, many awards and trophies, commendations, certificates, and accolades have been given to me on behalf of the Marching "100" Band and the university. Each one of them holds a significant place in my heart, as well as in my storehouse of esteemed treasures that are more valuable than fame, diamonds, or gold.

How do you measure success? Is it based on the number of wins versus losses? Is it based on the complexity of the task, or program? Is it based on how much support you received from others?

In my world of marching bands, the fans often determine who wins and who loses. And, at other times, a select group of my peers determines the success of my program.

THE SUDLER TROPHY

Winning or losing is sometimes a relative thing. There are so many constraints in the equation to succeed. Money, talents, university support, rules and regulations, laws, student and staff attitudes, talent, or lack of it by those who are participants, are factors that might limit band programs. All of us have to take what we have and work it, mold it, and sometimes pray for and about it. Even then, we cross our fingers. When we have done all that we believe we can do, then we put our faith in God, knowing that He will bring us through.

When the announcer introduces the Florida A&M University Marching "100" Band before a filled stadium of cheering fans, my staff, the students in the band, and I all know that it is showtime. We step out into our arena of competition and give it our all. Then, it's usually up to our fans to let us know if we have won or lost, succeeded or failed.

The FAMU Marching "100" Band wants to please its fans all the time. Every time it steps onto the field to perform, the Marching "100" wants to win.

Dr. William Foster and Mr. Louis Sudler

The band is so competitive that it wants to win even on the practice field. I believe that this is the attitude of a champion. It is this attitude that has earned us the respect of our audiences and the recognition that the band has received, nationally and internationally.

The Sudler Trophy is awarded annually to a collegiate marching band that is "of particular excellence and [has] made outstanding contributions to the American way of life." The award is made possible by a grant from Louis and Virginia Sudler of Chicago, Illinois. The John Philip Sousa Foundation administers the annual selection and presentation of the award.

The first recipients of the Sudler Trophy were the University of Michigan Marching Band in 1982, the University of Illinois Marching Band in 1983, and the Ohio State University Marching Band in 1984.

In December 1984, I received the following letter from Dr. Al G. Wright, president of the John Philip Sousa Foundation. The letter, dated December 17, 1984, is complimentary:

> Dear Bill:
>
> It is with a great deal of pleasure that I inform you that your fabulous Florida A&M Marching Band has been named recipient of the Sudler Intercollegiate Marching Band Trophy for 1985. Congratulations!
>
> This is undoubtedly the highest honor that can come to a university or college marching band in the United States. The three previous recipients of the Sudler Trophy are the University of Michigan Band for 1982, the University of Illinois Marching Band for 1983, and the Ohio State University Marching Band for 1984.
>
> At your convenience we will appreciate your sending us some B&W photographs of the band, the staff,

yourself; also, send some public relations material. The Sousa Foundation will announce this to the press next spring. We will keep you advised.

The presentation of the trophy should take place at a time and site of your own choosing. We hope it will be at a time when your marching band is on TV. We do request that it be at a time when there is not a visiting band present, which could be uncomfortable.

The Sousa Foundation will be pleased to visit your campus several weeks prior to the actual presentation in order to finalize plans and schedule. We will be in touch with you about this next April or May.

I know that with your experience and expertise that the 1985 Sudler Trophy presentation to your Florida A&M Marching Band will be the most brilliant and exciting to date.

Sincerely,
Dr. Al G. Wright
President
John Philip Sousa Foundation.

On October 26, 1985, the Marching "100," the FAMU family and I were humbled to receive the prestigious Sudler Intercollegiate Marching Band Trophy for 1985. Having been chosen the recipient of the Sudler Trophy has been described as "the highest honor that can come to a university or college marching band in the United States."

Left to right, The Honorable Bob Graham, Mr. Louis Sudler, and
Dr. William Foster

To be the recipient of the Sudler Trophy award, to walk or march
with such distinguished honorees, remains an accomplishment of
which we are very proud, not so much for ourselves but, most importantly, for our university and its community of supporters at home
and abroad.

I have been asked many
times, "Which of the awards
that you have received is most
cherished?" That's a tricky
question. Each award, no matter
how small or grandiose, is both
valuable and appreciated. Yet,
if I were forced to choose one
of many, I guess the coveted Sudler Intercollegiate Marching Band
Trophy would garner first place!

From a public perspective, the Sudler Trophy is considered the Heisman of marching band awards, one that any band director, band, and university would be honored to receive. More importantly, however, from a personal as well as a professional perspective, I cannot forget the invaluable services rendered to me by Mr. Edward Peters, a former member of the John Phillip Sousa Band, when I was just a developing musician and band director.

From left to right, Dr. Frederick Humphries, Governor Bob Graham, Mr. Louis Sudler, Dr. William P. Foster, Dr. Al Wright, Dr. Julian White, Mr. Leander Kirksey, Jr.

I recall that I was teaching in Springfield, Missouri, when I became intrigued with the very name, Sousa—because as you know, Sousa is top of the top drawer. Also, at the time, I had a positive attitude and was hungry for knowledge. I longed to study with Mr. Peters to gain knowledge of his various experiences with the Sousa band. He passed on a lot of pertinent tidbits, and I'm certain that I put many of t hem into my personal inventory.

Apparently, Mr. Peters, who lived in Springfield, also had a positive attitude, since he consented to allow me to study with him. Although he could have said I had a lot of nerve, or that he was retired and didn't wish to be pestered, he didn't. Contrastingly, he became interested that I wished to study with him and agreed to my request. He deepened my appreciation of detail, articulation, and dynamic contrast—basically subtlety and refinement. When I think of the experience, I realize that more than fifty years have passed. Still, there is a special affinity I have for the Sousa entity. Thus, to have progressed to the rank of Sudler recipient is a significant accomplishment for me.

I guess you're saying that's a long answer to a short question. Yes, it is—somewhat.

The Bicentennial
Bastille Day Parade

PARIS, FRANCE

O n the morning of January 16, 1989, I received a trans-atlantic telephone call from Dr. Jean-Paul Goude in Paris, France. I could not imagine why someone would be calling me from Paris.

Shortly after we greeted each other, I realized that Dr. Jean-Paul Goude, the Impresario, was inviting the Florida A&M University Marching Band to perform in the 200th Anniversary Bastille Day Parade. The parade would be held on July 14, 1989 in Paris.

Dr. Jean-Paul Goude speaks with Dr. Foster.

Dr. Jean-Paul Goude stated that the French government would pay all expenses incurred by the Florida A&M University Marching Band to include round-trip transportation between Talla-hassee and Paris, room and board for the entire trip, and incidentals.

As I listened to Dr. Goude, I could hardly believe what I was hearing. Yet my answer to Dr. Goude was a conditional yes, pending the approval by the university president, the state of Florida, and our federal government. These officials and organizations would have to approve such a momentous international venture.

After calculating the estimated cost of transportation and room and board for 250 band members to Paris, France, I dismissed the possibility of this adventure being realized.

Obstacles that immediately came to mind included the task of communicating with marching band members in May, June, and July, during the off-season for the marching band. The marching band was in its best form during football season or in the fall of the year. How was my staff going to get more than two hundred members of the 329-member band together to practice and do all the other things we would have to do to get ready for the trip?

We would need all band members on campus for practice for at least two weeks before departure for Paris. We would have to get official absences for band students who were enrolled in the summer session. Room and board arrangements would have to be made for those students not in summer school who we wanted to go with us on the trip. We would have to make certain that all passport requirements and other details were in order. Much had to be done, and there was not a lot of time to make it happen.

The cost would be overwhelming, at least to people like me who had problems getting enough money to pay the bus fare for the band to go just to a neighboring city in Florida.

The more I thought about the invitation, the more problems I had believing that we were really going to Paris. However, when Mr. Jack Lang, French Minister of Culture, transmitted a letter dated February 6, 1989, to Dr. Frederick S. Humphries, president of Florida A&M University, we had our official invitation to represent the United States of America during the French Revolution Bicentennial Commemoration. The unexpected, the unbelievable had happened.

The expenses of moving the band personnel, including chaperones and university officials, were borne by the French Government. Costs included round-trip transportation from Tallahassee to Paris as well as room and board—a value in excess of $500,000 and an average cost per student of $2200.

The Paris experience was exhilarating, a historic milestone and high honor for the band to be the official and sole representative of the United States of America in the Bastille Day Parade. We were privileged to assume the role of goodwill ambassadors of America.

It was a sensational thrill and experience for the FAMU band to be wildly cheered and applauded by two million or more enthusiastic and happy people along the Champs Elysees from the Arc de Triomphe to the Place de la Concorde, the route of the French Bicentennial Bastille Day Parade and Extravaganza.

Upon its return to Tallahassee, the FAMU Marching Band received extensive press coverage by the *Tallahassee Democrat*, numerous newspapers in Florida, and throughout the United States and the world. Photos and articles of the band appeared on the front pages of *The New York Times*; *New York International Herald-Tribune*; *Times of London*; and a centerfold in *Elle*, *Newsweek*, and *Time* magazines. Newspaper and magazine headlines described the FAMU Marching Band as "The hottest thing in Paris," "The sensational celebrities and stars of Bastille Day Parade," the "Super-band to star in Paris show," the "US birthday gift to France," the "Toast of Paris," and "America's band."

Two million spectators at the Bastille Day Parade and over five hundred million people on worldwide international television reviewed the band. It was a wonderful educational experience for our students to tour Paris; take a boat ride up and down the Seine River; and tour the Eiffel Tower, Louvre Museum, and Versailles.

I am proud of and elated at the super performance rendered by our band. The decorum, personal bearing, discipline, and responsiveness of its members were excellent.

The Paris trip, from its conception to its completion, was a great challenge. I believe that we must approach a challenge with a deep sense of wisdom and vision, commitment, daily practice of optimism, perseverance, dedication, and determination. We approached the Paris challenge with a strong work ethic, character, and personal bearing.

In order for these concepts to be imbedded in our youth, peak performance skills must be achieved—namely, internal control and responsibility (tough skin), the skill to plan and set measurable goals, a high level of self-worth, and mental rehearsal. Also needed is the visualization of desired outcome, the ability to accept feedback for self-correction, and the willingness to take risks.

It is recorded in the annals of history that ordinary people who achieved international recognition had all learned the basic skills of assuming total responsibility for their own motivation, the willingness to put in great amounts of time, energy, and effort, and to have an obsession with achievement of personal goals and objectives. Attention is called to the fact that appropriate verbal, written communication, and mathematical skills must be mastered.

The increased level of achievement leading toward the road of excellence is directly connected to basic performance skills. It is important that individual students at any level of ability accept the need and desire for high standards of academic achievement. In closing, the emphasis on excellence reminds me of the motto of the band, which focuses on qualities by which we live: highest quality of character, achievement of academics, attainment in leadership, perfection of musicianship, precision in marching, and dedication to service.

We were all very excited after returning from France on July 15, 1989. It was as if we had represented the United States of America in the Olympics and were returning victorious to the States. We were winners. It was as if we had been in a great battle or war and had returned triumphant to our shores.

Returning from what was almost a dream of unbelievable joy, we were trying to grasp the moment. I was so excited about what had happened to me and other FAMUANS that I had difficulty sleeping at night.

Once we had arrived in Tallahassee, Florida, congratulations began coming in from all over America. The Florida A&M University Marching "100" Band, if not already world famous, was now center stage. We were invited to appear on local and national television shows. It was a continuation of what had happened in Paris. While we were overseas, CBS, NBC, and ABC had the Marching "100" Band perform on their morning shows, simultaneously. To accommodate them, we had to split up the band into three units. When a band is made up of more than three hundred members, you can do that.

The city of Tallahassee welcomed us home with a downtown celebration on the grounds of the city hall. One speaker after another congratulated us. All of them were proud of the Florida A&M University Marching "100" Band. Their recognition made the band members, my staff, and me feel very good. The student members of the band were walking on clouds as the recognition and congratulations continued to come in.

Mr. Willard Scott and
Dr. William Foster

If this was an "era of good feelings," believe me, it was welcomed and appreciated.

Among the many public appearances I made upon my return was an address to fellow Rotarians in the Tallahassee and Northside Rotary clubs at the Tallahassee-Leon County Civic Center. This was what I told them about the Paris trip:

> Bonjour! I'm Dr. William P. Foster, and I feel like I
> am on top of the world. You now know I have been

to Paris, France. I thank you for the opportunity of presenting the Florida A&M University Marching "100" Band, ambassadors of the United States of America, at the Bicentennial Bastille Day Parade and extravaganza in Paris, France, on July 14, 1989.

It was an exhilarating experience, a historic milestone, and an honor for the 250 members of the Florida A&M University Marching Band to be the sole representatives of the United States of America in the French Bastille Day Parade and ceremonies.

The FAMU band was proud and privileged to have assumed the role of goodwill ambassadors of and for America.

I deem it an honor to elucidate on the opera-ballet Bastille Day Celebration that followed the parade in the Place De La Concorde in commemoration of the two-hundredth anniversary of the French Revolution.

After numerous telephone calls and exchanges of corre-spondences, the official invitation to Dr. Frederick S. Humphries, president of Florida A&M University, was received on February 6, 1989 from the Honorable Jack Lang, the French Minister of Culture. The Impresario, chief

administrator, and director in charge of all aspects of
the parade was Dr. Jean-Paul Goude. He was the
artistic director and creative genius who, along with
his competent staff, produced the Bastille Day Parade
extravaganza.

It was Jean-Paul Goude who decided that our band
play only the music of Mr. James Brown. Dr.

Goude also suggested that
the band create dance steps,
maneuvers, and routines
for the parade performance.
He said that the music of
James Brown represented the
embryo and psychic center
of popular jazz music in
America.

Jean-Paul Goude stated that
you cannot go anywhere
in the world where the rhythms and beat of Black
music and jazz are not present at discothèques or in
the concert halls—especially syncopation and jazz
rhythms. America has given two creative art forms
to the world. They are jazz and folk-country music;
the latter has the accompanying beat and rhythm of
the Black beat and jazz idiom.

Jean-Paul Goude's musical selections and suggested
routines were "dead on target" and absolutely
correct for the two million parade viewers. The people
along the parade route responded to the music and

routines of the FAMU band with great enthusiasm and emotion. The spectators danced, whistled,
clapped their hands, and smiled. At the parade run
through, due to popular reaction from spectators,
the FAMU Marching Band was moved from seventh
to tenth position in the parade. This was a great
honor for us.

The parade units were fantastic. They were very
beautiful and massive in size. Can you imagine
a French band of a thousand or fifteen hundred
African drummers and about as many Russian
dancers?

There were four staging areas that poured parade
participants into the starting location—the Arc de
Triomphe. The parade then proceeded down the
Champs-Élysées and into the Place De La Concorde
with an international worldwide television audience
of five hundred million. Huge throngs broke
through the police barriers to march along the side
and behind the band. Over a hundred thousand
spectators joined the band. As far as the eye could
see, there was a sea of people behind the band
during most of the parade.

The audience was the most appreciative, responsive,
enthusiastic, and excited we have experienced. The
scene was a combination of Times Square at New
Years and Mardi Gras.

As you know, the city of Paris is renowned as the "City of Light." Every parade unit was illuminated and every costume of the eight thousand participants was colorful and attractive to the eye.

The FAMU band was framed in front and in the rear with a replica of a stadium, including fans, American flags, break dancers, cheerleaders, and bright illumination. The parade was two and one half hours in length.

The French government provided a positive response to all of our requirements. Our educational experiences consisted of sightseeing tours in six fifty-passenger buses, visitation and guided tours of the Louvre Museum (Mona Lisa), Versailles, a boat ride on the famous Seine River, Notre Dame Cathedral, the Eiffel Tower, and shopping tours.

After viewing these facilities, one can understand why the French are such proud, patriotic, yet commanding people.

Mr. Oliver Lance stated that the French would have the surprise and shock of their lives at seeing and hearing the Florida A&M University Marching "100" Band. In part, that response would probably be related to the spirited nature of our band's performance. The military bands of Europe are very reserved and use a slow tempo to march and play music.

Most Europeans were unaware of the FAMU band. They were used to the strict military style and slow tempo of European bands. For them to see and hear a band that marches and executes drill and dance routines, while simultaneously executing fascinating movements with instruments, legs, and arms was a dramatic departure from that with which they were familiar. In comparison, the FAMU band with its faster tempos and fascinating and exciting marching maneuvers brought excitement to the parade spectator.

Members of the FAMU Band compare techniques with performers from the Russian Band.

Of great interest, also, was FAMU students' interaction with the Russian band student during break time. The students exchanged pins, cameras, shirts, sunglasses, and various souvenirs. They also interacted with the groups from Dakar, Senegal.

The French people were friendly and smiled a lot. They were kind and helpful in assisting foreigners, especially with those of us who tried to speak French. I am proud and elated over the super performance rendered by our band. The FAMU band joins me in extending thanks to the Northside Rotary Club for allowing us the opportunity to make this presenta-

tion relevant to our visit to Paris. I now bid you au
revoir. Viva la France. God bless America!

I'll tell you, the trip to Paris, France, was just what the doctor
ordered! Moreover, it was a great boost for Florida A&M University—and more than that, for the state of Florida. Truly, it was the
"icing on the cake."

All the post-Paris recognition was satisfying. Still, while I enjoyed
the celebration with the general public, there was an extra bit of excitement and enjoyment deep down in my bones for Black people. Every-

thing I could possibly do to help bring
some joy, some comfort, some feeling
of victory to Black people everywhere,
gave me an extra bit of satisfaction. In
everything I have done, I have wanted
to do it well before my people.

Having witnessed the struggle
of Black people, not only as a child
and as a student at the University of
Kansas, but even since then, it is exciting and particularly satisfying to
play a part in any activity that can bring joy to a people who continue
to struggle for equality in our country. Notwithstanding my joy for all
Americans, I know that African Americans and other Black people
everywhere are lifted just a bit higher by the work that is in progress
at Florida A&M University. I am extremely happy that I have made a
positive contribution to the growth and development of that work and
to the work of Black people.

Marching "100" in Presidential Inaugural Parades

The Florida A&M University Marching "100" Band marched in the 1993 and 1997 inaugural parades of President William Jefferson "Bill" Clinton.

It is always an honor for the Marching "100" to be invited to participate in a national event. Each time an invitation is extended to FAMU, it says that other people like what we do and that they want to see us perform. This kind of recognition causes us to work even harder to put on our best show the very next time we march. We hope that invitations to perform at the national level never stop coming.

"Everywhere we go ... People want to know ... Who we are." I have always liked that cheer. Everywhere the Marching "100" goes, people know about the band. They know that it's the world-renowned Florida A&M University Marching "100" Band.

After the second inaugural parade in 1997, an article entitled "Marching '100' Steals Show at Inaugural," written by Carol Rosenberg of the *Miami Herald*, is reflective of how our public responds to performances by the Marching "100":

People did the Macarena in the bleachers. They did the Macarena in the street. Even President Clinton poked stiff-as-a-rail Vice President Al Gore, as if to dare him, when Florida A&M's Marching "100" stole the show Monday by performing a screaming, sassy version of the dance down Pennsylvania Avenue in the Inaugural Parade.

"They invented band!" exclaimed Sheila Barnes, forty-four, of Mitchellville, MD., as she and her family watched in wonder as the orange-and-turquoise-clad band blasted by FBI headquarters in hour two of the largely ho-hum parade. "Words can't describe them," said Barnes, who was bored by one-too-many Sousa marches but stuck around for Florida A&M University at the urging of a friend. "They're current. They're fresh. They're up-to-date."

Or, as eight-year-old Talia Henderson of Adelphi, MD, put it: "They're awesome. That was cool!"

No one seemed to captivate the crowds—and then set them dancing—like the 329-member band that not so many years ago marched down the Champs-Élysées to celebrate Bastille Day.

"They're sharp!" shouted Sharon Pugh, forty-two, a grandmother, as she danced wildly in the stands. "They play the right music. They know how to dance to the beat. I love them. They are the only band here playing pop culture that the rest of us can relate to."

—Carol Rosenberg

FIRST LADY'S VISIT AT FAMU

First Lady Hillary Rodham Clinton visited the Florida A&M University campus in Tallahassee to drum up support for Democrats in 1996. She was right in step as she marched with one of the drum majors of the FAMU Marching "100" Band.

I considered it a great honor to have had the first lady visit our campus. It showed that FAMU and its supporters were valuable to the political process in this country. It also showed that our work at FAMU was appreciated, even by the president and first lady of the United States of America. Our students were being exposed to national leaders because of their work, their excellence, and their success.

First Lady Clinton's visit said to all of us that we were not alone, that we were being heard even in Washington, and that the sound of the Marching "100" was a good sound.

Slowing Down But Still Pushing Forward

In 1996, I began to feel tired. I was slowing down. However, I was caught up in my work at Florida A&M University and continued to push forward. I had an excellent staff working with me and felt that we could still get the job done. The Marching "100" Band was at the top of its game. Our fans were our greatest supporters. Still, it seemed that time was speeding up for me. The years were coming and going too rapidly.

The college football season from year to year kept my staff and me busy. Dr. Julian White was doing just an outstanding job of getting the band ready for pregame and halftime shows. The band shows were better than ever. More and more fans were filling the stands to see the band.

In recent years, the numbers of high school students participating in the Florida A&M University Summer Band Camp were on the increase. My staff worked diligently with the young people who attended the camp from all over the United States and the islands. Dr. Julian White oversaw our band camp and, as usual, he and the other members of my staff did outstanding work. With the availability of Marching "100" Band videos, junior high and senior high school students and their music directors were able to study the techniques of the Marching "100" more closely.

It was becoming normal to hear band-camp students talking about watching the Marching "100" Band on video. This gave us an incredible advantage. These young people wanted to come to our band camps to show us what they could do. Also, they wanted to learn how to do everything the members of the Marching "100" could do. Many of our band-camp participants became members of the Florida A&M University Marching "100" Band. Indeed, God was blessing us.

A Great Floridian

In early March of 1997, I received a letter from the Florida
History Associates on behalf of the Museum of Florida
History. In part the letter read: "Dear Doctor Foster: On
behalf of Florida History Associates, we are pleased to notify you of
your nomination as a Great Floridian. This honor has been bestowed
on eleven other individuals who have made notable contributions in
shaping the state of Florida as we know it today."

Well, I was honored to have been
nominated, and I accepted the honor
humbly but proudly. My committee would
also be responsible for planning a luncheon
or dinner for the honoree to be presented
publicly.

What was I going to do? How was I going to set up the committee that was required by the Florida History Associates? This was a problem, since I did not have the kind of support system at Florida A&M University that could help me meet the requirements of receiving this great honor.

My work continued. There was much to be done. The football season would begin in September. There would be many hours of toil before the Marching "100" would be ready for the first game. There was so much involved with getting ready for showtime and our pregame and halftime shows. The thought of all that work to do dwelled on my mind. Exhaustion became a resident in my being. It was getting more difficult for me to keep up with students in the band.

Dr. Julian White

My slowness was more noticeable to me, and, as I learned later, to others. I had become dependent on the other members of my staff. I knew that Dr. Julian White and the other members of my staff would prepare the band for the 1997 season. I was beginning to spend less time with the band and more time focusing on administrative duties. I could not have continued without an outstanding team of well-educated, trained, and considerate professionals.

We did get through the 1997 season. My team did another out-standing job. Sometimes, you forget to tell people how much you respect and appreciate their work, especially when you have worked with all of them for more than thirty years. My senior staff members were so much a part of every move I made. They had become my eyes and ears. Most of the time, they knew what I was thinking before I expressed myself. We were a team. We all had special roles to play, and most times we played them well. I appreciated and thanked them.

Senior band staff from left: Dr. Julian White, Associate Director of Bands; Mr. Charles S. Bing, Assistant Director of Bands; Mr. Carlos Mackie, Programs Coordinator; Dr. William P. Foster; Dr. Shaylor L. James, Professor of Percussion; and Mr. Lindsey B. Sarjeant, Arranger and Director of Jazz Studies and Commercial Music

In January 1998, I turned my attention to the Great Floridian program. All of us knew that this honor, although bestowed on me, was for all of us. Each time any of us who were on the band staff

received awards or some other honor relative to the Marching "100" Band, these things confirmed what FAMU and its supporters already knew: that together, we had something special and something of which we could feel proud. We were on top of the world, and we were not in a mood to come down or to let any others come to the top of the mountain with us.

Dr. Foster on the day of the Great Floridian proclamation.

Finally, the Great Floridian program began. It went well. The crowd was larger than expected. We all enjoyed the program. The spokesperson for the Florida History Associates, Dr. Melvin Stith, presented me with a special certificate and medal.

Mr. and Mrs. Foster.

Once he had finished his presentation, he invited me to address the audience. I had a prepared text. As I read it, my mind was more focused on the announcement written into my address than on other comments. I felt like I was floating through it all. When I got to the words concerning stepping down, I took a moment to breathe, and then I said it. It was one of the most difficult moments for me. After more than fifty-two years as director of bands and chairman of the Department of Music at FAMU, I was relinquishing the top job.

The announcement shocked most of the people in the audience. The person who seemed most surprised was my wife. She could not believe it. I had decided not to tell her before the program, because she might have had such an emotional reaction that she might not have attended the program. I knew that it was going to surprise her, but I thought that after she had a bit of time to think about it that she would agree with my decision.

Mr. Charles Bing, Dr. Julian White, Mr. Lindsey Sarjeant, and Dr. Shaylor James were in the audience. They were surprised and realized the passing of the torch was taking place. The other members of staff, present and past members of the Marching "100" Band, and other friends and associates were also surprised; some were in a state of shock.

I had finally found the strength to make the move that I had been considering for some time. Although it was a difficult thing to do, it was the right thing for me to do.

When I got home that evening, I did my best to relax. I knew that my wife was still trying to adjust to my announcement and that it would be a while before she would be at ease with the decision. I hoped that she would be all right with it.

I suppose I did get a few hours of sleep that night. The next morning, I awoke with the stark reality of what had happened the night before. I really had announced that I would step down on July 31, 1998. Now that the announcement was made, I knew that it would take some time for me to make the adjustment of not being in charge.

The Dr. William P. and Mary Ann Foster Foundation

The Dr. William P. and Mary Ann Foster Foundation is the realization of a dream I have had for years. I have wanted to financially help students who were members of the FAMU Marching "100" Band since my coming to FAMU. To that end, I have given thousands of dollars to truly needy FAMU students. I have worked endlessly to get financial support for them from large and small corporations and from private citizens. Yet, regardless of how I have tried, I have never been able to do enough.

The students who participate in the FAMU Marching "100" Band come from every type of socioeconomic background. These students bring their outstanding talents to our table. FAMU and the state of Florida take advantage of their talents to make millions of dollars. Yet, these students receive little, if any, financial support in return toward their college education. Their only rewards are the joy of being active participants in the band and the experience gained. We must ask: Are these rewards enough for services rendered? Are these rewards enough when the state of Florida makes millions of dollars from the efforts of these students? After more than fifty-five years of working with young people, I think they deserve better treatment and support. They deserve substantial support.

The Dr. William P. and Mary Ann Foster Foundation has been created to help do a better job of supporting the truly needy students at Florida A&M University.

The Dr. William P. and Mary Ann Foundation is a conduit for all of us to reach out our hands to the truly needy FAMUans who participate in the Marching "100" Band and to others. With the support of many, The Dr. William P. and Mary Ann Foster Foundation, Incorporated, was founded and is a 501 (c)(3) nonprofit organization.

THE MISSION OF THE DR. WILLIAM P. AND MARY ANN FOSTER FOUNDATION

The mission of the Dr. William P. and Mary Ann Foster Foundation focuses on the financial support for truly needy students who participate in the Marching "100" Band and others. I want the foundation to focus on students in the FAMU Marching "100" Band. The foundation will work to direct all of its attention on the financial needs of these students. It's my hope that with your support, the foundation will make a difference.

Too often, out-of-sight means out-of-mind. There is so much going on in all our lives until, sometimes, we just do not have time for other people. At least, that is what we have convinced ourselves to believe. We sometimes forget that it does take a village to raise a child. Economically challenged students should not be forgotten at FAMU. They need us. If we remember them, they will remember what we did for them and will not forget the next generation. That's my abiding hope and prayer.

The Dr. William P. and Mary Ann Foster Foundation will help us to remember and, hopefully, all of us will continue to support our young people. Too, we must keep in mind that under the direction of the FAMU band staff, the students have made the Florida A&M University Marching "100" Band, if not the best, one of the best-performing marching bands on earth. Its halftime performances at football games are well known and attended. During football season in the fall, some schools against whom FAMU plays football demand that the Marching "100" Band comes with the football team to perform at pregame and at halftime shows. These schools know that their fans want to see the Marching "100" Band as much as, or more than, the football teams.

When the Hundred steps onto the football field, everyone knows that it's showtime. The crowd waits with great anticipation as the announcer begins. "And now, the world famous Florida A&M University Marching '100' Band!" With that introduction, the Hundred begins its show as the crowd comes to its feet amid a deafening ovation. The crowd stands to greet the Marching "100" Band with great expectations—expectations that are always fully, emphatically realized, I might add!

Our young people from all over the Americas continue to enroll at Florida A&M University to become members of the Marching "100" Band, as they pursue an education. They are the ones who perform year after year for tens of thousands of cheering fans. They are the ones who make us proud. They are the ones the Dr. William P. and Mary Ann Foster Foundation seeks to assist. With your help, we will make a difference.

There are many different social groups, cultures, and races in the United States. As a result, it is critical that Black America be able to maintain its identity and heritage. Florida A&M University and the other Historic Black colleges and universities are valuable contributors to the healthy growth and development of the Black community. This community needs these colleges and universities, as well as their related personalities. Future generations of Black Americans and others will want to know about the legendary Dr. William P. Foster of Florida A&M University and the world-famous FAMU Marching Band.

The foundation has begun reaching out to its public. The Dr. William P. and Mary Ann Foster Foundation is the people's foundation and will be there for the truly needy at Florida A&M University. Join us. We must tackle or embrace this venture together.

To contact the foundation:

Dr. William P. and Mary Ann Foster Foundation
P.O. Box 5393
Tallahassee, Florida 32314
www.drwpfosterfoundation.org
E-mail: info@drwpfosterfoundation.org

Eminent Scholar

On November 1, 1996, during homecoming week, Florida A&M University sponsored a banquet in honor of my fiftieth year of service at FAMU. Symphony No. 50—Fostering Excellence—was the theme for my golden-anniversary celebration.

Ceremonial "Passing of the Baton" performed during the first home football game in September 1998. The baton was passed from Dr. Foster to Dr. White

During the celebration, the university president announced to the audience that I would be the first person to sit as eminent scholar in the Foster-Edmonds Endowed Chair at Florida A&M University. I appreciated the comment; however, I was not ready to leave my current responsibilities, not at the time, anyway.

On July 31, 1998, nearly two years later, I stepped down as director of bands and chairman of the Department of Music at Florida A&M University. I stepped down with the understanding that I would remain on the teaching staff and be given the emeritus title for the positions that I had vacated.

On August 8, 1998, the university presented me with a new contract and elevated me to the position of eminent scholar. As had been previously agreed, the university invited me to sit in the Foster-Edmonds Endowed Chair. I gladly accepted. It was my understanding at that time that I would remain in the Foster-Edmonds chair until I retired. This expectation resulted from the last meeting I had with the university president before announcing that I was stepping down from the positions I held.

During my first year as holder of the Foster-Edmonds Endowed Chair, I spent most of my time trying to set up my office. I needed a secretary and certain pieces of office equipment. I had to clarify budget and other administrative concerns before I was assigned a senior secretary or received office equipment. Some of the problems I encountered were due to the fact that I was the first scholar to sit in the chair.

During my first year in the chair, I received minimal support from others at Florida A&M University. It seemed that I was having extreme difficulty trying to communicate my needs to FAMU officials. I concluded that I would have to find a more effective way of getting assistance with office concerns. Otherwise, I was going to have a lonely and difficult time getting my work done.

After trying numerous times to get support from others at the university, it became obvious to me that I would have to set up my office by myself. I was holder of the Foster-Edmonds Endowed Chair, but I had no real support from the university. By this time, I was seventy-eight years old. I thought, "How am I going to do all this work by myself?" Since no one from Florida A&M University had offered assistance to me, I did what I thought was best to get the personnel and equipment needed to operate my office.

My ultimate plan was to write a book about my life's work while sitting in the Foster-Edmonds Endowed Chair. To this end, I spent countless hours pulling together all the materials on my work. There were hundreds of articles, letters, certificate of awards and other documents that needed to be moved from my house to the office. I spent time summarizing and writing about my professional experiences.

Finally, in January 2000, Ms. Terry "Kibibi" Rouse, a senior secretary, was assigned to me. After Ms. Rouse was in place, I began moving my personal files from my house to the office. I took the opportunity to brighten the office a bit by hanging personal paintings, pictures, certificates of award, and plaques. Shelving was installed in my office. One and one-half years after becoming the holder of the Foster-Edmonds chair, my office area began to look like a professional office.

My secretary helped me organize and type materials. Her spirit, attitude, patience, and willingness to do whatever was necessary to get the job done were encouraging to me. Her positive behavior helped to move the project forward. She was quite helpful.

Although we were able to gather much information on my life's work, neither my secretary nor I knew how to write the kind of book I had in mind. So, realizing that I needed technical support, I put in a request through the office of the provost and vice president for academic affairs for a technical assistant and a writer. Shortly thereafter, I was informed that there was no budget for my request. With that information at hand, I had to do something else to get the work done. I decided to reach out beyond the boundaries of the university for help. This support came with a cost that was paid from the salary I received as eminent scholar and holder of the Foster-Edmonds Endowed Chair.

Just before the end of my second year in the endowed chair, I was notified in writing by the university that my position as holder of the endowed chair would end on August 7, 2000. I was shocked and discouraged. This meant that I had about six months to finish my work and to close shop. Until I had received that notice, I had thought I would be in the chair until I decided to vacate it. I wondered what I was going to do.

Sometimes when you are disappointed, you do the best you can to put a positive light on the situation. Thus, I began to rationalize. I reasoned that since I was not getting any younger—perhaps it was time to stop. I had already begun to wonder how much longer the Lord would bless me with good health. I reasoned that unless the university was going to give me the chair for life, so that I might continue to be a goodwill ambassador for the state university system of Florida, that perhaps it was about time for me to step down from the chair and turn in my retirement papers. There was just one problem. I needed more time to finish writing about my life's work. I had always believed in completion.

Along with the notice informing me that I would have to vacate the endowed chair on August 7, 2000, the university presented me with a one-year contract, effective August 8, 2000, to remain on the teaching staff of the FAMU Department of Music.

THE PEN VERSUS THE SWORD

I made an offer in writing to the university concerning the endowed chair and my work. In response to my written request and a few words of support from friends of mine, FAMU allowed me to remain in the Foster-Edmonds Endowed chair until August 2001. The additional year would give me more time to finish my work and prepare myself to leave the campus. I just hoped that God would continue to bless me with reasonably good health through it all. I would be eighty-two years old in a year.

Working on this book was good for me. It made me look into those backrooms of my mind. Before I began to write the book, I was so busy planning for tomorrow that I had little time to remember yesterday. Now, although I was still busy with tomorrow, doing a good job required me to remember yesterday.

There were so many events and situations, so much information from which to choose. I knew that I was going to be successful. *The Man Behind The Baton* would soon be a reality. I could hardly wait for it to be in print.

REPRESENTING FAMU

Besides working on the manuscript of my life's work, I was busy attending programs to receive awards and other honors. Although these programs were in honor of my work, I knew that they honored all of us who were involved in the Department of Music and the Marching "100" Band. When I received any honor, I received it for the university. When I was invited to participate in any program, I did it on behalf of FAMU. After more than fifty-five years of service for FAMU and the state of Florida, whatever I did reflected on them. So I wanted to always do my best as one of their representatives.

MY RETIREMENT RECEPTION

While all this was taking place, I submitted my retirement papers to the university in June 2001. The time was near for me to leave FAMU after more than fifty-five years of service. I was about to change careers.

Sure, I thought about retirement. How would I handle it? What was I going to do as a retired person? I supposed I would soon figure it out.

Working on the book helped me to focus on my life's work— and on just how much time had passed since I graduated from the University of Kansas. As I filled out the required papers for my retirement, I did all I could to convince myself that it was time to go. But first, I wanted to finish *The Man Behind The Baton*.

On Thursday, August 2, 2001, the FAMU Department of Music held a reception in my honor. My wife and I attended.

This reception was the last event for me as an active member of the FAMU music staff. Dr. Julian White, chairman of the department and director of bands, presided over the short program. Mr. Charles S. Bing, associate director of bands; Dr. Shaylor James, assistant director of bands; Mr. Johnny Williams, Jr., music department librarian; Mr. Shelby Chipman, assistant to the director of bands; Dr. Arthur Washington, dean of the College of Arts and Sciences; and Mr. Timothy Barber, head drum major of the Marching "100" Band, were also in the program. A number of choral students and members of the marching and symphonic bands participated in the program. The comments of all the participants and the musical selections by the students were meaningful and dear to my wife and me. Some of the people cried as they remembered all that we had done together. A number of the staff had worked with me for more than thirty years. We were like a close family. I appreciated what they had to say. All of them were very special to me, and I knew that I was going to miss them. God had been good to me, and He was still looking favorably upon me and mine. "Thank you, Lord," I whispered.

RETIREMENT

My secretary, Ms. Rouse, and I began packing boxes and preparing to vacate my office about a week before the reception. On August 6th, the day before my retirement, I realized that I still had much to do before leaving the office. Since, at my retirement reception on August 2nd, the dean of the College of Arts and Sciences had announced that my office would remain my office for as long as I wanted, I decided that it would be all right for me to move the boxes to my house on Friday, August 10th.

I was home. Retired. A dream realized.

A Great Challenge

Today, the band student is expected to develop and exhibit a positive attitude toward achievement and to develop the highest level of ability in music and in marching rehearsals and performances. The student is expected to develop a positive attitude toward learning and striving for perfection in all things.

The band student is required to give the best efforts to attain the upper percentile of his or her ability. Rehearsals will be enjoyable and meaningful experiences as a result of the student's desire to improve. Student enthusiasm for achievement must be high. Without question or doubt, enthusiasm will ignite the power within each band member to strive for excellence.

It is a true saying that "to whom much is given much is expected." I am referring to the intellect and mental ability, the character and personal bearing, and the talent and musical proficiency. I implore the student to strive to develop his or her total self into a productive citizen and a person of dignity and worth.

Also, I strongly urge the student to be receptive to learning, suggestions, and instructions so that he or she keeps an open mind. I ask students to do two specific things: look on the bright and good side

THE MAN BEHIND THE BATON

of life and develop a positive attitude toward responsibilities, obligations, and assignments. Learning, accomplishments, achievements, and attainment come to no one as gifts. Only perseverance, hard work, high ideals, self-sacrifice, ambition, and faith can bring success to an individual. Neither special favors nor sentimental apologies for the past can develop character and encourage progress. The student is charged with the challenge, urged to make the most of existing opportunities, and encouraged to strive for achievement.

Each student must have a belief in being the best, to practice strong work ethics, to develop healthy and wholesome character traits and fine personal-bearing habits. In order for these concepts to be imbedded in the inner-self, high-performance skills must be active—namely, internal control and responsibility. The student must also develop a tough skin and attitude. He or she must develop the skill to plan and set measurable goals and objectives and to achieve a high level of self-worth and self-esteem.

Further, each student is asked to assume responsibility for his or her own motivation to succeed. To develop excellence, the student must be willing to put in great amounts of time, energy, and effort, thereby attaining and achieving personal goals and objectives. The student is reminded that written communication and mathematical skills must be mastered. With the focus on excellence, the student is encouraged to consider the band motto of the Florida A&M University Marching Band as his or her personal guide. This motto sets forth qualities by which band members live. It guides their thoughts, actions, and lives.

MY NICKNAME

It was some time before I realized I had a nickname. However, I began to notice that when I would drive up to the band practice field that the band students would begin humming the siren sound of a police car. It was not long thereafter that I discovered my nickname was "The Law." In other words, they were letting everyone know, "Here comes The Law. We better tighten up."

Because I am a perfectionist in terms of precision in marching and in music performances, it was not unusual for me, upon hearing repeated errors in executing a difficult phrase or passage in the music, to ask those students to please "lay-out" for effect. This meant that they would not continue to play until they had corrected the errors. Many students attest to the fact that this statement caused them to work harder toward improving themselves through frequent visits to the practice rooms.

Today, I am often referred to as "The Maestro," "The Law," and

"The Legend." I like all three of the names. They "fit" me.

The future of our youth in this changing world is dependent in part on how we as contributors to our community and society can assist youth in becoming high achievers. This is a great challenge.

Band Pageantry

THE DREAM OF A LIFETIME
THE CREATION OF THE BOOK

Band pageantry is a spectacular performance, executed by a marching band. It is designed to entertain the public at pregame, halftime, and postgame periods of football games.

My book, *Band Pageantry*, was written for directors of bands at junior and senior high schools, colleges, and universities as well as for instrumental music majors at the undergraduate and graduate levels.

In writing it, I attempted to establish a guide through which the educational and cultural values in band pageantry may be realized. It is assumed that the reader of *Band Pageantry* possesses a working familiarity with the organization of the marching band, together with the knowledge of participation skills.

Band Pageantry presents basic-drill and precision-drill concepts. It provides step-by-step instructional techniques for developing the band into a precision marching and musical organization.

The book details ways to plan band pageantry. There are instructions on resources for themes, planning procedures, day-by-day format, equipment, facilities, charting, script, and announcer. It includes complete halftime band pageant plans with routine sheet, script, and storyboard including formations and video and audio chart for television. There are charts and formations with animation and glossary for band pageantry. It provides information about drum cadences of unusual interest. Drum cadences are proven audience pleasers.

Band Pageantry is filled with concepts of still and animated formations and use of resource groups: musicianship, arranging, know-how on such things as travel, public relations, budget and requisitions, instruments and uniforms, a sample day-by-day schedule of rehearsals, pre-drill band rehearsals, administrative aspects of band pageantry, and the various roles of personnel in developing band pageantry.

Band Pageantry is concerned with the philosophy that band pageants can be educational and functional musical experiences if they are based upon ideas of interest to people and if they are produced with a proper balance between accepted standards of music and of entertainment. To be truly significant experiences, pageants should embody educational and cultural values, which have meaning for both the band members and spectators. Underlying the pageant should be a philosophy that is exemplified in terms of music as well as in the maneuvers by which the drama is portrayed. The creative process involved suggests new resources from which bandleaders may draw materials and ideas for thematic development.

The proposals set forth in *Band Pageantry* constitute a means through which interaction may take place between the band and other areas of the school. There is a strong probability that members of the school staff will agree to assist the band director in working out this approach to band pageantry. Thus, the marching band will have a unique opportunity to utilize not only sources of knowledge and ideas but also to receive active assistance from the school. This plan of guidance for band pageantry is suggested with the hope that it will help to elevate the quality of marching band performances.

The seed for the book was planted during my conversation with Dr. Donald M. Swarthout, dean of the School of Fine Arts, in May 1941, prior to my graduation from Kansas University, and it is my hope that it will remain available to future generations of band directors and music students. It's also my hope that it will continue to serve as a guide for the creation of outstanding pregame, halftime and postgame marching band performances. *Band Pageantry* is a proven guideline to successful marching band performances. It is about entertaining rather than merely playing a few musical selections while marching from one end of the football field to the other end.

Religion and Philosophy

When I think about what is most important to me, two things come to mind. The first is my spiritual relationship with God, and the second is my relationship with my family. Certainly, my career has meant much to me, but without God and my family, my career would be meaningless. There is much satisfaction in thanking God for His blessings and for directing my life. There is much satisfaction in seeing and feeling the joy of family members after working day and night to get a particular detail right. There is so much satisfaction in knowing that your wife supports your efforts and is proud of what you do. It's satisfying to know that your family unit is working together in love. God and family are the foundation of a healthy life.

When I am asked if my attitude toward family resulted from my spiritual upbringing, I am not sure of the answer. I suppose my answer will always be the same: "I don't know."

I realize that there is a certain relationship between how one views the family and God. It is just the way I was raised; the way the people in my community lived; the way the grown-ups acted in my community; the way all these things came together when I was a child, along with genetics, I suppose, that caused me to feel and act as I do.

I am the youngest of four children. I had two brothers and a sister. Vondorus, my oldest brother, was twelve years older than I; Dorothy, my sister, was eleven years older; and Delphos, my older brother, was eight years older.

My mother and the children lived with my step-grandfather and grandmother until I was five years old. My maternal grandfather died before I was born. I think that my grandmother married my step-grand-father just before I was born. I did not realize that my step-grandfather was not my grandfather until I was an adult.

When I was five years old, my mother got a house. My brothers and sister moved with my mother into that house. However, I stayed with my grandmother and step-grandfather. I stayed with them because the house in which my mother had moved was too small for all of us. There was not enough bedroom space. Besides, I liked living with my grandmother. The other house was just three blocks away. As a result, we were together, just as we were before Mother moved to the other side of the street.

Mother and Father were separated before Mother moved. When I was seven or eight, my mother married my stepfather, Mr. Tucker. He was a good man who treated my mother and her children well. I liked him. My father died in Chicago, Illinois, when I was twelve years old.

Although there were divorces and remarriages in my family, the family unit was very important to all of us. Father and Mother provided the basic needs of life for us. Love, reward, and punish-ment were there, just as were food, clothing, and shelter. I was always encouraged to do my best—to excel. I was always encouraged. My self-esteem increased with time. My grandparents also worked with my parents to assure my success.

RELIGION

My step-grandfather and grandmother were members of the African Methodist Episcopal (AME) Church in Kansas City, Kansas. I attended Sunday services with them but do not recall any formal ceremony to accept their belief. It was normal for me to go with my grandmother to church services since I lived with my grandparents.

My stepfather and mother were members of the Baptist Church and the AME Church. I loved all my parents.

When I left home to attend college at the University of Kansas, as I remember it, I had not joined, or accepted, any particular spiritual belief. However, I believed in God and in Jesus Christ, His Son.

My family had always been Christian based. We had lived according to the principles of that belief. As a child in that environment, I learned from others in my family. My personality resulted from their influences and from all the things which happened in that environment at the time.

While at the University of Kansas, I participated in the Baptist Youth Ministry. I did not become a Baptist but went to their services because it was convenient for those Black students who attended the University of Kansas.

After graduating from the University of Kansas, I worked at Lincoln High School in Springfield, Missouri, from 1941–1943. I was not involved with a particular church during that time. However, I took the school choir to various churches about once a month to perform during their services.

I accepted the Fort Valley State College job in 1943 and remained there for one year. While at Fort Valley, my second son, Tony, was born in the infirmary on April 28, 1944. Mary Ann, my wife, began attending Catholic Sunday School with Patrick, my older son. Patrick was born on December 23, 1940. Fort Valley State later became Fort Valley State University.

In 1944 I accepted a music position at Tuskegee Institute as director of the band and orchestra. I was there from 1944–1946. The institute held a nondenominational church service every Sunday morning and chapel every Sunday evening. It was mandatory for students to attend these services. We marched to church service each Sunday morning. The school band led the way, playing "Onward Christian Soldiers." The service was quite formal. The institute chaplain was in charge of the service. He would normally bring the sermon. Sometimes, other distinguished ministers were invited to the institute to preach.

The chairman of the Department of Music and director of the choir at Tuskegee Institute was the great Dr. William L. Dawson. He and the choir participated in church and chapel services.

Chapel attendance was mandatory for students. Come to think of it, chapel service was similar to church service with one difference: lay people were given the opportunity to speak during chapel.

I was director of band and orchestra at Tuskegee. I was responsible for the marching and concert bands and the orchestra. It was my job to get the band ready to perform the march to church service and the orchestra to perform at Vespers.

Our Sunday morning marches to church services were routine. Nevertheless, our presentation was very important to me, even at that early point in my career. I always wanted the students to do their best during each service.

While at Tuskegee, although I was very involved in church and chapel programs, I did not formally accept the teachings of any particular group.

In 1946 I left Tuskegee Institute to become director of bands at Florida A&M College. In the summer of 1949, I was appointed chairman of the music department at FAMC. Once at FAMC, my family began attending church services at St. Michael's and All Angels Episcopal Church. We have been faithful members of St. Michael's and All Angels Episcopal Church since 1947.

After my confirmation, I served St. Michael's Episcopal Church for many years as lay reader. I served as reader of the Scriptures and prayers to the people. I served as director and coordinator of the church's annual musical for the community. I rendered service and made significant contributions to fund-raising activities. These efforts made it possible for the church members to make lasting enhancements to church buildings, furnishings, and equipment.

PHILOSOPHY

In 1975 the high school band directors of Tallahassee, Florida, sponsored a banquet in my honor at the Holiday Inn. The guest speaker was the Honorable Leroy Collins, former governor of Florida. I received a request from Governor Collins before the banquet for a list of things that identified my character and philosophy of life. After some thought, I sent him the following outline that I referenced as my philosophy of life.

My personal outlook on life:

    1. I take a positive outlook on life.

2. I look for the good and quality assets in people, things, and places.

3. I have and possess great faith and confidence in my fellow man.

4. I believe in assisting and helping those people who are less fortunate than I.

5. I always look to the pleasant things in life and in my association with people.

6. I look forward to a better tomorrow far above the horizon.

My philosophy on getting things done:

1. Think, survey, and procure an overview of the things to be done, which include the setting of goals and objectives.

2. Gather all information and knowledge of the things to be done.

3. Organize and outline the things to be done.

4. Evaluate and set up procedures of planned work; make a thorough analysis of the same.

5. Set up a timetable of work to get the job completed and work actually accomplished.

6. Put the plan into action to get the job done.

7. Follow through on all details to see and ensure that the things planned are executed and completed in a satisfactory manner.

8. Continue to believe in the work ethic.

Myself as a person:

1. I believe in the institution of the family.

2. I stand for good character (personal bearing, loyalty, decorum, manners, speech, dress, honesty, and highest regard for the rights of my fellowman).

3. I am satisfied with nothing but the best in quality, non-material and material. I like to enjoy the good things of life.

4. I am a perfectionist; therefore, everything I am associated with or do—duties, responsibilities to be performed—my philosophy is to excel and do the best I can in achieving excellence. I believe in perfection.

5. I have a high regard for competence, people, and organizations of high performance and excellence.

6. My life from early years was shaped and molded in terms of excellence and achievement of performance in all endeavors.

7. I am a devout believer in God and religion and often look above for advice, guidance, and counsel.

8. I am interested in the well-being of my fellowman. I enjoy being of service to assist and to improve the lot of people.

9. I am a confirmed believer in being a team member in all endeavors.

10. I am a workaholic, as my energy to work is almost endless.

11. I enjoy working day and night if my services are needed to complete a task.

12. I expect no rewards for my work, as the things I do are done because I wish to do them without thought of reward or thanks.

Noteworthy Contributors
to the Legacy

DR. WILLIAM H. GRAY, JR.

President, Florida A&M College

President Gray employed me as a band director for the express purpose of developing a band that would put FAMC on the map. He established a budget for the Florida A&M College Band to be used to set up a scholarship program for the marching and symphonic bands, to recruit talented students, to financially assist students in receiving a college education, and to employ qualified and competent instrumental teachers. He supported efforts for the marching band to accompany the football team to other campus football games.

REVEREND MOSES GENERAL MILES

Dean of Students, Florida A&M University

I express my thanks and gratitude and appreciation for Reverend Moses G. Miles for the role he played, along with Dr. William H. Gray, Jr., in contacting me at Tuskegee in the fall of 1945 and making a sales talk for me to come to FAMC.

I also think kindly of Rev. Miles' generosity in making financial aid available to band students who were in dire need of assistance in order to remain in school during the late 1940s. I recall Rev. Miles' financial assistance to band students in the 1950s and 1960s when there was no one else to whom band students could turn in their quest for work-study jobs for their survival in college.

ALONZO SMITH GAITHER

Athletic Director and Legendary Head Football Coach,
Florida A&M University

Coach Gaither was the number-one supporter and promoter of the Florida A&M University Marching Band. Also, Coach "Jake" Gaither was the number-one booster of the Marching "100." He encouraged and supported the marching band's trips to other campus football games, especially in Florida.

DR. GEORGE W. GORE, JR.

President, Florida A&M University

I am personally grateful to Dr. Gore for recommending and supporting my application for a fellowship from the Rockefeller General Education Board for two years of graduate studies for the doctoral degree at Teachers College, Columbia University 1953–1955. Dr. Gore was a strong supporter of the instructional program of the Department of Music.

DR. FREDERICK S. HUMPHRIES

President, Florida A&M University

Dr. Humphries is credited with the numeric growth of the university during his presidency from 1985–2001, a period of sixteen years. During his administration, the enrollment of the university increased from five thousand students in 1985 to more than eleven thousand in 2001. Also, during his presidency, the university was selected as the college of the year, 1999–2000, and ranked high in the recruitment of academic scholars.

The Department of Music and university bands benefited from the increase in student enrollment during this period. President Humphries was awarded the American Bandmasters Association's Edwin Franko Goldman Award as a result of his support of the FAMU Band Program.

I express appreciation and gratitude to Dr. Humphries for authorizing the Athletic Department and sponsors of promotional football games to finance all expenses of the FAMU Marching "100" Band for pre-game and halftime shows. These arrangements included the FAMU band being included in the football-game contract.

In addition, I am grateful to Dr. Humphries for awarding me the honorary doctor of humane letters degree and granting me emeritus status as chairman of the music department and director of bands. He also appointed me as the first recipient to hold the Foster-Edmonds Endowed Chair from August 1998 to August 2001.

During President Humphries' administration, the music building was renovated, a new band building was completed, and a new marching band rehearsal drill field with an irrigation system, lights, storage area, and observation towers was constructed. I am appreciative for those enhancements to our music program at Florida A&M University.

DR. MALON C. RHANEY, DR. LEEDELL W. NEYLAND, AND DR. AUBREY M. PERRY

Former Deans of the College of Arts and Sciences,
Florida A&M University

These three deans supported the programs of instruction in the Department of Music. They had positive roles in its growth and development.

DR. LENARD C. BOWIE

Dr. Bowie was the first graduate of Florida A&M University to be employed on the faculty of the Department of Music. Dr. Bowie served as associate director of bands and coordinator of instrumental music from 1959–1976. I thank Mr. Bowie for his professional contributions to the FAMU Band Program.

DR. JULIAN E. WHITE

Assistant and Associate Director of Bands,
Florida A&M University

Dr. White ushered in the use of the computer to plan pregame and halftime shows by the Florida A&M University Marching Band. His service was commendable because of his loyalty, dependability, commitment, dedication, integrity, and talent.

I am grateful for the ingenuity of Dr. White in his competence in learning the operation of the computer to program the design of formations, multi-drills, and staging of dance routines.

The utilization of the computer was a great time-saver in the structure of the band's pregame and halftime shows, as well as in a two-minute routine in front of Macy's in New York City, which was nationally televised at Thanksgiving from 1980–1989.

I recommended Dr. White to be my successor as chairman of the Department of Music and director of bands at Florida A&M University.

MR. CHARLES S. BING

Associate Director of Bands
Department of Music, Florida A&M University

Mr. Bing was appointed instructor and assistant director of bands in September 1960. He is the senior member of the faculty of the Department of Music and band staff. He performed outstanding service as proofreader and editor of all-important communications and reports of the Department of Music and university bands.

I commend Mr. Bing on his ability to evaluate and analyze improvements that enhance performances. I commend and thank him for his creativity in the writing of scripts for the symphonic band concerts—the scripts for the announcer of pregame and halftime shows performed for more than four decades in Tallahassee, as well as in other cities throughout the United States of America.

MR. LINDSEY B. SARJEANT

Music Arranger
Department of Music, Florida A&M University

Mr. Lindsey is the person responsible for the sound of the Florida A&M University Marching Band. Mr. Sarjeant is the arranger of the music performed by the band. He tailors the arrangements to fit the instrumentation of the band. His creative scoring brings out the best sound from the band. His creative arranging of the bass line, counter line, and harmonies results in greatly enhanced tones.

I commend him for styling the FAMU band sound through his creative arrangements of music for the band's pregame and halftime shows. The distinctive arrangements by Mr. Sarjeant personify the "FAMU Band Sound." For more than three decades, he was an outstanding arranger for the FAMU band.

DR. SHAYLOR L. JAMES

Director of Percussion
Department of Music, Florida A&M University

Dr. James has selected the best personnel for the percussion section. He has developed leaders for the sections of percussion instruments for the last thirty years. During Dr. James' tenure as director of percussion, he has done an excellent job of tuning six to eight different percussion instruments (snare, tenor, bass, timbales, quads, and such). Dr. James also does a remarkable job of preparing a forty-eight- to fifty-six-member percussion section. Dr. James strives to keep the volume of the percussion section under the sound of the band. His famous saying is "Percussionists are musicians, too."

MR. DONALD BECKWITH

Storekeeper, Equipment Manager, and Inventory Officer Florida A&M University, Department of Music and University Band

Mr. Beckwith's dependability and reliability in the performance of his job responsibilities and assistance to request have been most valuable to me personally. His performance in the issuance and collection of hundreds of musical instruments, pieces of equipment, and other supplies enables all areas of the many ensembles to function throughout the year.

I am grateful for and appreciative of his services. I would have been severely handicapped in the performance of my duties without the valuable services provided by Mr. Beckwith.

MR. JOSEPH "JOE" BULLARD

The Voice of the Hundred

Mr. Bullard began serving as an announcer during his junior year at Florida A&M University. He has continued to furnish color to the script of the pregame and halftime shows on and off campus for more than three decades. During this time, Mr. Bullard has only missed a few performances.

I am thankful to Mr. Bullard for his excellence as the announcer for the world-famous FAMU Marching "100" Band. One very important thing that he has taught us is that a world-famous band also needs a world-famous announcer. His voice for the last thirty years has been the "Voice of the Hundred."

MS. GLORIA JONES

Secretary,
Department of Music, Florida A&M University

Ms. Jones was a loyal, committed, capable, and dependable office employee. She rendered significant service as a receptionist, typist, keeper of records, filer, and producer of office work. She did an excellent job of interacting with the public and university students.

MS. TERRY "KIBIBI" ROUSE

Secretary

I am indebted to Ms. Rouse for her competence and expertise. She was invaluable to me as we set up my office for research. She was of great help to me and to the other members of my team as I wrote *The Man Behind The Baton*. I am grateful to Ms. Rouse for services rendered to Florida A&M University and me.

DR. INEZ Y. KAISER

Owner,
Dr. Inez Y. Kaiser and Associates Public Relations Firm

Dr. Kaiser was the first promoter and corporate sponsor on behalf of the Florida A&M University Marching Band. Dr. Kaiser established a scholarship, held dinners honoring the FAMU Marching "100" Band in Miami, Florida, during the Orange Blossom Classic (OBC), sponsored cars in the OBC Parade, and provided citations and such for the FAMU band. Dr. Kaiser actively supported the band from 1952 through 1975. I am most grateful to Dr. Kaiser for her support of the Marching "100" Band.

DR. VITO PASCUCCI

Former Chairman of the Board and CEO,
G. Leblanc Corporation

I am highly impressed with the intellect, creativity, vision, leadership, ingenuity, wisdom, and philanthropy of Dr. Vito Pascucci.

It was my pleasure and honor to meet and converse with Dr. Pascucci for the first time in 1968 at the Southern Division of the National Association for Music Education's National In-Service Conference in Mobile, Alabama. Since our initial meeting, I have been a goodwill ambassador of the G. Leblanc Corporation. The Florida A&M University Marching Band and the Florida A&M University Symphonic Band have been the recipients of promotional instruments from the G. Leblanc Corporation for thirty-five years.

From left to right, Dr. Julian White, Dr. Vito Pascucci, Mr. Leon Pascucci, Mr. Lindsey Sarjeant, and Dr. William P. Foster.

Without this support, neither of our bands could have relished the instrumentation we enjoyed. I am indebted to Dr. Pascucci for his philanthropic gifts to the FAMU Marching Band and the FAMU Symphonic Band from 1966 to the present time.

Mr. Leon Pascucci, Vito's son, has succeeded his father as president of the G. Leblanc Corporation.

DR. WILLIAM D. REVELLI

Director of Bands Emeritus, University of Michigan

Dr. Revelli was my role model. I revered him as a musician, coordinator, lecturer, writer, and speaker. Dr. Revelli was the founder of the College Band Directors National Association (CBDNA), the organization where I served as national president from 1983–1985.

Dr. Revelli nominated me as president of the American Bandmasters Association (ABA) at its national meeting in New Orleans, Louisiana, in March 1994. I was elected president of the ABA for the 1994–1995 term.

When I was president of CBDNA from 1983–1985, Dr. Revelli credited me with organizing and administering the best convention in the organization's history. He presented me to the membership of ABA at the opening sessions of the 1966 convention at Northwestern University, Evanston, Illinois.

MR. HENRY FILLMORE

Great Bandmaster and Composer,
Marching "100"

Mr. Fillmore and the "100" made history at the 1947 Orange Blossom Classic football game in the Orange Bowl Stadium in

Miami, Florida, before an audience of forty thousand spectators. There were twenty thousand Whites on one side of the stadium and twenty thousand Blacks on the opposite side of the stadium.

Midway through the second quarter of the football game, the announcement came over the public address system that Henry Fillmore would conduct the FAMU Marching Band from the stadium stands in one of his famous marches, entitled "Americans We."

The officials stopped the football game. Mr. Fillmore conducted the band, becoming one of the first Whites to conduct an all-Black band. The spectators gave Henry Fillmore a standing ovation and thunderous applause. The officials then resumed the football game.

DR. SYBIL C. MOBLEY

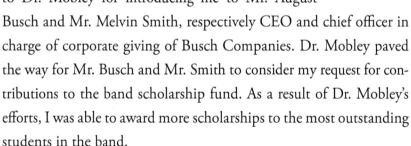

Dean of the School of Business and Industry (SBI), Florida A&M University

Dean Mobley has been very supportive of the band program at FAMU. I am deeply indebted and grateful to Dr. Mobley for introducing me to Mr. August Busch and Mr. Melvin Smith, respectively CEO and chief officer in charge of corporate giving of Busch Companies. Dr. Mobley paved the way for Mr. Busch and Mr. Smith to consider my request for contributions to the band scholarship fund. As a result of Dr. Mobley's efforts, I was able to award more scholarships to the most outstanding students in the band.

Thank you, Dr. Sybil Mobley, Mr. August Busch, and Mr. Melvin Smith, for the significant financial contributions from the Busch Companies to the FAMU Band Scholarship Fund.

MR. RAY CHARLES

International Singer/Entertainer

Mr. Charles has been a great supporter of the Florida A&M University music program. I am most appreciative to him and his business manager, Mr. Joe Adams, for the establishment of the Ray Charles FAMU Band Scholarship Fund. Ray Charles has made several substantial contributions to this fund through the years. The most recent gift was presented to me at the 1998 Summer Commencement Exercises at FAMU.

I commend Mr. Ray Charles for his philanthropic giving to the Florida A&M University Band.

MR. ROBERT E. FOSTER

Director of Bands,

Kansas University (my Alma Mater)

When my wife and I returned to the University of Kansas to receive the Distinguished Service and Achievement Award at the 1971 commencement exercises, Mr. Robert Foster and his wife, Becky, were our hosts.

During my term as president of the American Bandmasters Association, our 1994 annual convention was held at Kansas University. Mr. Robert Foster served as host for the convention. Again, he received my wife and me warmly. His hospitality was welcomed and appreciated.

DR. PAUL V. YODER

Outstanding Composer and Conductor

Dr. Yoder was a goodwill ambassador to Japan, and he's the person who encouraged and inspired me to write my book, *Band Pageantry*. I am indebted to Dr. Yoder for making the initial contacts with Hal Leonard Music, Inc., the publisher of *Band Pageantry*.

Dr. Yoder was instrumental in promoting me as clinician and guest conductor on a national scale. He gave a strong boost to my professional career.

COLONEL EUGENE W. ALLEN

Director,

United States Army Band

Colonel Allen sponsored and invited the FAMU Symphonic Band to Washington, D.C., to appear in a joint concert with the United States Army Band in Constitution Hall in the winter of 1979.

Colonel Allen also accepted my invitation for the United States Army Band, the Male Chorus, and the Herold Trumpets to present a concert in Lee Hall at Florida A&M University.

It has been my pleasure to be guest conductor of the United States Army Band in Constitution Hall in Washington, D.C., at the Music Educators National Conference in 1980 in Miami Beach, Florida, and at national conventions of the American Bandmasters Association.

DR. JOHN M. LONG

Dean of the School of Fine Arts and
Director of Bands Emeritus,
Troy State University

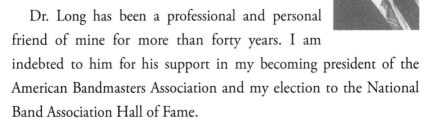

Dr. Long has been a professional and personal friend of mine for more than forty years. I am indebted to him for his support in my becoming president of the American Bandmasters Association and my election to the National Band Association Hall of Fame.

I thank Dr. John Long for the compassion, empathy, and kindness shown to me in times of great need in my work as director of bands at Florida A&M University. I am grateful and thankful for my friendship with Dr. Long.

DR. AUBREY M. PERRY

Dean of the College of Arts and Sciences,
Florida A&M University

Dr. Perry was a compassionate administrator who attempted to assist me in every way with problem solving and other matters of concern.

I appreciated his compassionate attitude and advice as he assisted me with personnel and budgetary matters. I appreciated his letters of recommendations on my behalf for several prestigious state of Florida awards.

THE HONORABLE ALFRED LAWSON

State Senator, Florida

State Senator Lawson and I lived across the street from each other for a number of years. He was a good neighbor and is a good friend. After serving eighteen years as a state representative, Mr. Lawson was elected state senator.

I have been a supporter of State Senator Al Lawson for more than twenty years. I am grateful to him for being a sponsor of bills in the Florida House of Representatives and the State Senate that resulted in several proclamations and resolutions being presented to me through the years. He also sponsored a reception in my honor in July 1985. In the fall of 1989, then-Representative Lawson presented me to the House of Representatives and awarded me a plaque honoring me as director of the FAMU Marching Band on its performance in France at the Bastille Day Parade.

I am forever indebted to Senator Lawson for his support of Florida A&M University, its Department of Music, the world-renowned Marching "100" Band, and me. His support has meant so much to me and the other members of the FAMU family.

DR. LEEDELL W. NEYLAND

Professor of History Emeritus
Former Dean of the College of Arts and Sciences
Vice President of Academic Affairs
Florida A&M University

Dr. Neyland was my supervisor during his tenure as dean of the College of Arts and Sciences. I was favorably impressed with his leadership style and professional competence.

Dr. Neyland was extremely helpful to me in adjusting or solving personnel and budget matters in the FAMU Department of Music. During his administration, he offered practical answers to concerns that I encountered as chairman of the Music Department.

MR. VICTOR GAINES

Student Photographer,
Florida A&M University Bands

Mr. Gaines continued to capture the activities and personalities of the band for a number of years after graduating from FAMU.

I am indebted to Mr. Gaines for taking hundreds of photographs of the band that are chronicled in the book *America's Band of Legend, A Pictorial Collection on Bands at Florida A&M University*, and in numerous other publications. I am most grateful to Mr. Gaines for his contributions in capturing the legacy of the FAMU bands in photographs.

MR. KEITH POPE

Official University Photographer,
Florida A&M University

Mr. Pope was the university photographer during my tenure as director of bands and chairman of the Department of Music at FAMU. I wish to thank him for the many photographs he took of the university symphonic and marching bands for a number of decades. Many of the band pictures that he shot have appeared in university yearbooks, the FAMU *Strike Magazine*, and many local and state newspapers. Thanks to Mr. Pope, people who have never visited the campus of Florida A&M University have come to visualize and love the Florida A&M University Band.

MR. CHESTER L. WILLIAMS

Outstanding Sculptor, Visual Arts Faculty,
Florida A&M University

I wish to thank and commend Mr. Williams for the bust of me that is displayed in the foyer of the Foster-Tanner Music Building at FAMU.

MR. ALVIN HOLLINS, JR.

Mr. Hollins is a talented and creative writer and editor of first-class football publications at Florida A&M University. I extend my hand and deepest thanks to Mr. Hollins for his outstanding articles on the FAMU Marching "100" Band and me that appeared in the FAMU *Strike Magazine* and the annual FAMU Football Guidebook.

DR. REBECCA WALKER BROWN STEELE

Dr. Steele was on the faculty of the Department of Music as a teacher of voice and director of the secondary choral group when I joined the music department on June 1, 1946.

Upon my appointment as chairman of the music department in 1949, there was a vacancy for the position of director of the college choir. In September 1949, I appointed Dr. Steele to that position.

I express my thanks and appreciation to Dr. Steele for her preparation of the FAMC musical groups for musical selections performed by the college and university choirs and the symphonic band for special occasions. Such occasions included visits to the college by the State Board of Control (later the Board of Regents) and renditions of special programs and concerts on and off campus.

Dr. Steele did an outstanding job of preparing the college/university choirs for performances with the university symphonic band. She also did a commendable job as chairman of instruction for choral music.

DR. S. RANDOLPH EDMONDS

Chairman of the Department of Speech and Drama,
Florida A&M University

One of the things Dr. Edmonds and I had in common was that our offices were located on the east and west sides of FAMU Lee Hall Auditorium, respectively.

Dr. Edmonds was a noted playwright and professor of speech and drama. I called upon him for assistance in writing the script for the FAMC Marching Band pregame and halftime shows. I also called upon him to identify and provide a FAMU student to serve as the announcer of our pregame and halftime shows. He was of great help to me at home and at off-campus football games where the FAMU band performed.

Since we were colleagues in the area of fine arts and our offices were located across the stage from each other, we were in daily contact with each other. We became friends. I am greatly indebted to Dr. Edmonds for his assistance and support, which began in the fall of 1946.

MRS. DOROTHY L. WILLIAMS
MR. EDDIE JACKSON
MRS. SHARON SAUNDERS

Staff Members, Public Affairs and Public Relations
Office Florida A&M University

These professionals published numerous articles about the Marching "100" Band. I would like to express special thanks for their publication of articles on the FAMU Marching "100" Band's participation in France's Bicentennial Bastille Day Celebration. I truly thank each for a super job.

MR. EDWIN W. PETERS

Former Cornet Player,
John Philip Sousa Professional Band

Mr. Peters took me on as a cornet student and tutored me on the basic elements of musicianship from 1941–1943, in Springfield, Missouri.

I am deeply indebted to Mr. Peters for helping me on my journey in life. I owe him big thanks for imparting the basic music fundamentals of performance of the John Philip Sousa Band and its director, John Philip Sousa. Mr. Peters tutored me in private instructions and used a book embracing the fundamental techniques of musicianship. These principles were used with my beginning band at Lincoln High School with amazing results. The rest is history and is exhibited by the miraculous success and musical performances by the FAMC (1946–1953) and FAMU (1953–1998) marching and symphonic bands and by guest-conducting engagements with high school, college/university, and service bands throughout the United States of America.

Again, thank you, Mr. Peters, for your professional tutoring.

MR. FRANK GIHAN

Administrator,

McDonald's All-American High School Band

I am forever thankful and grateful to Mr. Frank Gihan for his role in the decision of the McDonald's Corporation to appoint me the director of the McDonald's All-American High School Band in September 1980. As administrative officer of the McDonald's band, his approval of my operational plans for the band paved the way for its outstanding success.

MR. GASTON O. SANDERS

Director,
Sumner High School Band and Orchestra

Mr. Sanders was my high school band director at Sumner High School from 1934–1937. I am indebted to Mr. Sanders for guiding my career into music as a band director.

Upon entering Sumner High School in September of 1934, I enrolled in band. During the fall of 1934, Mr. Sanders appointed me as student director of the Sumner High School Band and Orchestra. This appointment enabled me to develop musically in tuning the band and orchestra, as well as in conducting music numbers of both organizations. As student director, I developed techniques of leadership and knowledge of the music score.

Mr. Sanders gave me instruction in playing the violoncello. This experience enhanced the development of my ear in tuning organizations and in the perception of the singing tone. Playing the violoncello improved my hearing and established my ability to perceive the singing tonal sound forever. These competencies carried over into my work with marching and symphonic bands. Therefore, Mr. Sanders had a major role in the development of my career as a band director and as a conductor!

MR. DAVID J. MONTROIS

Vice President,
Merrill Lynch, Tallahassee Office

I am most appreciative and grateful for the competent and prudent investment suggestions and guidance of Mr. Montrois, my financial advisor.

MR. WILLARD SCOTT

NBC's Today Show Weatherman
and Author of America Is My Neighborhood

Mr. Scott was the host for two performances each year of the 104-member McDonald's All-American High School Band. I directed the band at Rockefeller Center just prior to Thanksgiving each year from 1980–1989. I appeared with Mr. Scott in two short interviews each year during these national telecasts. The Florida A&M University Marching Band and I were also featured in Mr. Scott's 1987 book, *America Is My Neighborhood.*

THE HONORABLE LEROY COLLINS

Florida State Representative, 1940–1954
Governor of Florida, 1955–1961

Governor Collins was a man of principles and moral character. He cared about the welfare of all Floridians. When I think about politicians who were supportive of the civil rights of Black Floridians, Governor Collins' name is at the top of my list.

Governor Collins was a progressive and innovative politician who had a special passion for education and human rights issues. However, he was limited in his efforts because the Florida legislature was filled with segregationists who could not envision integration as it is today. Still, Governor Collins stayed the course and was a giant among Floridians in his efforts to do the right thing. His efforts as state senator and as governor of Florida made a difference to me and to the community of people served by Florida A&M University. His political position on various educational and human rights issues was invaluable in the positive growth and development of the Black community. He is one of my legends.

THE HONORABLE BOB GRAHAM

Florida State Representative, 1966–1970
Florida Senator, 1970–1978
Governor of Florida, 1978–1986
United States Senator, 1986–2005

Senator Graham became a supporter of the Florida A&M University Marching Band when he was a child. Do you remember the Orange Blossom Classic football game? It was held in Miami, Florida, for many years. The Orange Blossom Classic parade took place on Saturday morning before the game. Senator Graham, as a child, always stood on the parade route and watched the Marching "100" go past. He fell in love with the FAMU Marching Band and has been a great supporter of FAMU and its band throughout his adult years.

Senator Graham has taken the lead on a number of political issues facing FAMU and its band. He has been there for us numerous times. I believe that he should be included in all that we do at Florida A&M University. He has proven himself to be fair and a strong supporter of FAMU and the community of people it serves. Senator Graham cares about FAMU and about what we feel is right.

Senator Graham has shown me, time and time again, that he recognizes the work that I have done at FAMU. I have always sought his council and have considered his direction whenever it was given to me. He has been a friend to the Marching "100" Band and to me for a long time.

THE MAN BEHIND THE BATON

THE HONORABLE
CARRIE P. MEEK

United States Congresswoman from Florida

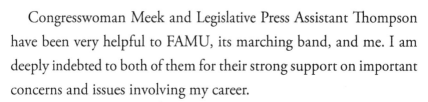

MR. TOLA R. THOMPSON

Legislative and Press Assistant

Congresswoman Meek and Legislative Press Assistant Thompson have been very helpful to FAMU, its marching band, and me. I am deeply indebted to both of them for their strong support on important concerns and issues involving my career.

DR. JEAN-PAUL GOUDE

Impresario,
200th Anniversary Bastille Day Parade, Paris

Florida A&M University and I will be forever thankful and grateful to Dr. Goude for selecting the FAMU Marching "100" Band to represent the United States of America in the historic Bastille Day Parade on July 14, 1989, in Paris, France. This event presented the FAMU Marching "100" Band to the world via international broadcast. The estimated viewing audience on worldwide television was five hundred million people.

ATTORNEY DOUGLAS MANNHEIMER

I am indebted to Attorney Mannheimer for legal counsel on matters of career concerns. I value his pragmatic courses of action, his contacts in regards to legal matters, and other concerns.

Attorney Mannheimer is a great admirer and supporter of the FAMU Marching "100" Band. He has supported the band and me for years.

DR. MARY W. ROBERTS

Chairman of Piano
Department of Music
Florida A&M University

Dr. Roberts graduated with a bachelor of music degree from the University of Kansas. She has been a close friend of the Foster family for many years.

Dr. Roberts' husband, Mr. Willie Roberts, a mathematics instructor at Florida A&M University, is a graduate of FAMU and a former member of the FAMU Marching "100" Band. Also, Dr. Roberts' son, Mr. Wilkie Roberts, is a FAMU graduate and a former member of the FAMU Marching "100" Band.

Dr. Mary Roberts has contributed much to the success of the Department of Music and its symphonic/concert orchestra. She has been a strong supporter of my efforts at FAMU. Her work ethic and loyalty are commendable.

Reflections on
Dr. William Patrick Foster

DR. OSIEFIELD ANDERSON

Professor of Mathematics
Florida A&M University

Each era in human history is marked by a few men who see beyond the horizons of other men; men who exhibit a spirit of philanthropy that other men never feel; men who have the courage to ask the daily question, "Why do I get up in the morning?" and the wisdom to answer that question; and men who hear and respond to a call to duty that other men never hear. Approximately four decades ago, I was fortunate—indeed blessed—to meet one such a man in the person of Dr. William Patrick Foster.

I reflect in pleasant memories on the many years I have known and worked with Dr. Foster in academia. During these years, I had the opportunity and privilege to confabulate with him numerous times. And each time we conversed, I was delightfully lifted to a new and higher dimension of a sense of purpose of life and living. His conversations were never trite and ordinary but were always teeming with words of wisdom, words of encouragement, and words of hope and of goodwill. Even his humor had within it a lesson of didactics.

No one can gainsay the fact that Dr. Foster's academic attainments in education and in music are unduly significant and have catapulted him into an orbit of national and international acclaim shared by only a few. Only a precious few men and women have impacted education as has Dr. Foster. However, as significant and noteworthy as his educational and musical achievements are, these are not what make him Dr. Foster. Had he been a ditch digger, a carpenter, or a farmer, he would have excelled to heights of greatness in these endeavors because his greatness is "something within." Dr. Foster is much bigger within than without. Knowing the "inner man" and the position Dr. Foster holds in the "hall of greatness," one can clearly see that Plato was right: "What we see is a shadow cast by that which we do not see."

As I reflect on that phase of Dr. Foster's life that I witnessed, I see a man whose life was and is a wonderful sermon for us—a man whose life has taught us how to live in deeds and not in years, in feelings and not in breaths, and how to count time by heart throbs and not by numbers on a dial.

I recall very vividly the first time that I saw Dr. Foster direct the Marching "100." When he stepped upon the platform and raised his arms, there was "magic in the air." And there could be no doubt that such a magnificent performance as the audience beheld was from within. We live in two worlds: an inner and an outer. And it was certain that Dr. Foster was a good citizen of his inner world and it reflected beautifully in the outer. I have had the opportunity to watch him conduct the band numerous times since that first majestic moment. And each time is always like the first time—inspirationally and enjoyably wonderful.

The concepts of past, present, and future make us three-dimensional beings in the outer world. And for most persons, these concepts act as a gauge to measure who we are, where we are, and what we are. However, the inner world is neither confined to the ticks of clocks nor to the turning of pages of a calendar. And it is in this inner world, and indeed in one's mind and heart, that he discovers his "true self," which knows neither youth nor age, neither a beginning nor an ending, and no yesterday or a tomorrow—only today. We have dual citizenship, and Dr. Foster's good citizenship in his inner world is what makes him great in the outer.

I have a niece who is a graduate of Florida A&M University. She was a music major, and on one occasion she wanted to discuss some matters of concern to her with Dr. Foster. She came to me and apprised me of her desire to talk to Dr. Foster but stated that because of his musical fame and notoriety, she was afraid to talk with him. However, I was able to assure her that Dr. Foster was even bigger in heart than he was in worldly fame.

Consequently, I was able to allay her fears to the degree that she made the appointment to see him. After her visit with Dr. Foster, she came to my office in smiles, laughter, and serenity of mind and said, "Anderson, I talked with Dr. Foster, and he is the nicest person I have ever talked to."

In reflection, I see a man in the person of Dr. William P. Foster who has served as a beacon for more than five decades, pointing young people in the direction of a better life but particularly to young Blacks who without his guidance might never have had the opportunity to seek that better way.

As I reflect on the almost forty years that I have known Dr. Foster, I feel certain that he is the kind of personality that motivated Rudyard Kipling to describe a man in the following words in his poem "If—" :

If you can keep your head when all about you
Are losing theirs and blaming it on you,
If you can trust yourself when all men doubt you,
But make allowance for their doubting too…
If you can talk with crowds and keep your virtue…
Or walk with Kings—nor lose the common touch …

In summary, reflecting on my relationship with Dr. Foster, I see a life well lived. I see a man who has risen to the top rung of the ladder of success. But, most importantly, I reflect on the life of a man who has risen to the top rung in human compassion. Dr. Foster has raised kindness to a new and higher level, knowing that kindness is the music of goodwill to men. And that like the Psalmist David, on Dr. Foster's metaphorical harp, the smallest fingers in the world can play Heaven's sweetest tunes on earth. To him, benevolence is the only action of a man's life that assures happiness. And he exhibits this godly quality in every action of his being. Dr. Foster has immortalized himself through the countless lives he has touched. Countless generations, yet unborn, will one day rise up and call his name blessed.

"I dare do all that may become a man.
Who dares do more is none."
—Shakespeare

DARYL D. PARKS

Past Student Body President and Former
Member of the FAMU Board of Trustees

From the time I first saw Dr. William P. Foster as a high school student at Walt Disney World in Orlando, I was amazed with what he represented. When I became a student at Florida Agricultural and Mechanical University (FAMU), I saw his greatness at work. As a lawyer, I had the privilege of representing him. Simply put, he was a class act in all aspects of his life. We in the FAMU community owe him a great debt of gratitude for the substantial institution impact he had on who we are as a university community.

THE HONORABLE BOB GRAHAM

The 38th Governor of the State of Florida - 1979 to 1987;
United States Senator - 1987 to 2005

Pat, your selection as a "Great Floridian" by the Florida History Associates on behalf of the Museum of Florida History formalized what many of us have known for well over fifty years. Your unrelenting appreciation for excellence has been chronicled by many awards, recognitions, and documentaries.

Since 1946, your creative genius and leadership of "America's Band of Legend" at Florida A&M University has served as a blueprint for other band directors across the country. It is no wonder that you are affectionately referred to as "The Maestro," "The Legend," and "The Law." In fact, we would be hard pressed to measure the full impact you have made on our state and the world through the universal language of music.

Through your guidance and direction, countless students have experienced the rewards and benefits of hard work. You have been credited with revolutionizing marching band techniques and reshaping the world's concepts of collegiate marching bands. Many, experiencing success of their own, have become a major part of your legacy. It is a rich legacy and a special part of our nation's past, present, and its journey through the 21st Century. It is often said that music is the international language. This makes you, Dr. Foster, an ambassador of sound and dance and of the international spirit.

Let me tell you a personal story. Ten years ago, when I was governor, I asked Dr. Foster and the Marching "100" to join me on stage for a surprise appearance at the annual press skits in Tallahassee.

The annual press skits are interminable. They go on forever. Fortunately our part of the show was early in the evening. When the curtain went up, the Marching "100" filled the auditorium with sound; the audience was on its feet clapping and dancing. The place was pumped! The band finished its show with its normal dance line out of the auditorium. Half the audience followed it. They understandably figured that the show was over—that nothing could follow the Marching "100."

Dr. Foster, anyone who has heard your music from Bragg Stadium to Carnegie Hall—from inaugural to Bastille Day, anyone who has picked up a trumpet in your brass section, or any of the millions who have seen you and the "100" perform—we are all honored to be in your band of followers.

We thank you and your lovely wife, Ann, for fifty years of service. Allow me to extend my sincere best wishes to you.

THE HONORABLE LAWTON CHILES

Former Governor of Florida

Dr. Foster has spread the word of music for the past fifty years. Dr. Foster has influenced generations of students. He is known as the Father of the world-renowned Marching "100" Band, which began with a sixteen-piece band and a dream. The Marching "100" is a symbol of excellence. It has performed around the world for sports fans, presidents, and international dignitaries alike. Thank you, Dr. Foster, for your hard work, your dedication, and your perseverance. You have been a true role model. You have touched the lives of many Floridians, and you have made FAMU proud. Congratulations.

CHARLES REED

Chancellor of the State University System of Florida

Congratulations to you, Dr. Foster and Mrs. Foster, for fifty years of absolutely fantastic service to the state of Florida and to Florida A&M University. Dr. Foster, when you have the reputation of having the best band in the world, I can only say that you have brought great prestige and great visibility to our university system. We thank you. We also want to thank Mrs. Foster for being your support base these many years because we all know you could not have done it without her help. We know the dedication that you have put into Florida A&M University. Once again, thank you for what you do for all the people in this great nation of ours and for giving so many young people the opportunity to be number-one in the world for a marching band.

DR. JAMES AMMONS

Provost and Vice President for Academic Affairs,
Former President of Florida A&M University

On behalf of the university and the entire academic community of which Dr. Foster has been a contributing member for fifty years, I am honored to bring greetings to him and to Mrs. Foster during this special celebration of his outstanding service. Dr. Foster's distinguished career as a music educator and as director of the famed Marching "100" Band and symphonic band has enhanced the image of Florida A&M University on the state, national, and international scenes. Because of his outstanding record here at FAMU, Dr. Foster has served as president of the major music associations, including the prestigious American Band Masters Association. Additionally, Dr. Foster is a professor, writer, researcher, and scholar who has left many legacies for us to follow as we strive for "excellence with caring."

Dr. Foster, we appreciate all that you have done for the university. We sincerely hope that you will have success in your future endeavors.

DR. JULIAN E. WHITE

Associate Director of Bands (1964–1998)
Director of Bands and Chairman of the Music Department
Florida A&M University (1998–2012)

I am indeed honored to reflect on my experiences with Dr. William P. Foster. I first met Dr. Foster when I was a band student in the Duval County Honor Band. Dr. Foster served as the guest conductor. It was indeed an honor for me since I had heard so much about him from my sister and brother who had played in the Florida A&M Band.

Upon high school graduation, Dr. Foster offered me a scholarship to attend Florida A&M University—another honor for me. I participated in the marching band and the symphonic band. I served as the flute section leader, the saxophone section leader, and as head drum major. This gave me a chance, as a student leader, to work very closely with Dr. Foster.

After I graduated from Florida A&M University and returned to Jacksonville, Florida, where I served as band director at William Raines High School, I still had very close contact with Dr. Foster. Subsequently, he offered me a position as associate director of bands at the University. I was honored that he would think enough of my ability to ask me to work beside him. I have had a wonderful experience as I have watched him share his knowledge and his love for the world of music with the band staff and students. Congratulations.

DR. SHAYLOR L. JAMES

Professor of Percussion,
Florida A&M University

It is indeed an honor for me to have this opportunity to express my sincere congratulations to Dr. William P. Foster for fifty years of exemplary service to the university, the Tallahassee community, the nation, and the world of music as director of bands at FAMU.

For the past fifty years, Dr. Foster has had the opportunity to touch the lives of thousands of men and women through his dynamic leadership and musicianship. I am fortunate to be in that number.

I am a by-product of the 1960s. During this period of turmoil and change, Dr. Foster remained true to his ideas and his pursuit of excellence. When I think of Dr. Foster's work during the '60s, I think of character, discipline, precision in marching, and perfection in musicianship. These were some of the attributes that made Dr. Foster and the Marching "100" stand alone.

Dr. Foster always managed to remain calm in the heat of battle. He was a master psychologist who knew how to achieve optimum results. For instance, say we were rehearsing for a show on Friday evening and an individual had problems learning the routine. Dr. Foster would not panic. He would calmly beckon that person to the sideline and calmly say to him, "Young man, how about standing on the sideline and seeing how this formation looks without you?" And the show went on.

In symphonic band rehearsals, some individuals would have a problem playing a closing run or an opening phrase as precisely as Dr. Foster wanted it. Again, Doc would not panic. He remained calm. He would simply tell those individuals to lay out for effect, and the show went on. Dr. Foster is known to some as "The Law" and to many as "The Maestro."

I became sectional leader of the percussion section, and subsequent to my graduation in 1964, I was hired to teach percussion and work on the marching band staff. The thirty-two years that I have worked under Dr. Foster's leadership have truly been rewarding from every conceivable standpoint.

Fifty years is a long time to do anything. To maintain the level of excellence that Dr. Foster has done through his career is remarkable. In the words of an old Negro spiritual, "Let the work I have done speak for me." Doc, your fifty years of excellence certainly speak for you. May you continue to foster excellence for many more years. Hubba, Doc.

DUNCAN MOORE

President,
Tallahassee Memorial Regional Medical Center

Dr. Foster, it's a privilege for me to join with many others in congratulating you and Mrs. Foster on the occasion of your fifty years of service, not only to Florida A&M but to this city, this state, and this nation.

As you know, I am in a civic club with you—a club that has retired governors, university presidents, a majority of the members of the Florida State Supreme Court, and many other notable people. It seems about once a month that the chair recognizes you for some additional contribution that you have made to this city, this state, and to Florida A&M. On more than one occasion, I have thought that perhaps no one in his chosen field of endeavor has succeeded like you. No one! No governor, no senator, no supreme court justice in his or her chosen field of endeavor has achieved the degree of accomplishment that you have.

Few people in this country or in this world, literally, have made the contribution to their chosen fields that you have in yours. The impact that you have had on music, on bands, and on leadership is nothing short of phenomenal. Our city, our state, and our country have received international recognition as a consequence of it.

So, it's a pleasure and a privilege for me to join with many others in lauding you and your wife for fifty years of major accomplishment and contributions to this city, state, and nation. Congratulations.

CAROL DADISMAN

President and Publisher,
Tallahassee Democrat Newspaper

Bill, you and the band you have created and sustained and the music program that you have created and sustained over these fifty years have brought excitement and thrills to millions of people all over the world. More than that, they have brought opportunities for thousands of young people coming through the programs to make them better musicians and better citizens.

You and Mary Ann have been great citizens of Tallahassee. You have provided so much to our community—so many contributions.

So it's a great pleasure for me on this occasion of your fiftieth anniversary to join in this salute to you and Mrs. Foster and thank you for all that you have done for Tallahassee, Leon County, and Florida.

DR. FREDRICK HUMPHRIES

The eighth President of Florida A&M University
from June 1, 1985 to December 31, 2001

Individuals become geniuses because they have the ability to see beyond the horizon. Their vision is so great that they are not limited to the range of perception of ordinary mortals. It is this capacity to invent and innovate that has lifted William "Pat" Foster into his own orbit of excellence as the premiere architect of creative performances by marching bands in the country.

Your career as director of bands and head of the Department of Music at Florida A&M University has been so outstanding that I think genius is the only appropriate expression for your monumental achievements over half a century of service. Congratulations, Pat.

DR. AUBREY PERRY

Dean of the College of Arts and Sciences,
Florida A&M University

On behalf of the college, I extend to Dr. William P. Foster and his lovely wife, Ann, our sincere congratulations for giving us fifty years of distinguished service as our director of bands and chairman of the music department. Florida A&M University, the state of Florida, and indeed, the United States of America are fortunate to have had the services of Dr. Foster over these years.

Dr. Foster, as your colleague, I am truly proud to be able to tell you that Florida A&M University is a better place because of your distinguished leadership. Congratulations, and may you work toward another fifty years of service to FAMU and our nation.

JOSEPH L. WEBSTER, SR., MD.

More than fifty years ago, in 1946, William Patrick Foster came to Florida A&M University as director of bands. When I was a child, all the people in my hometown of Monticello were excited about that great FAMU Marching "100" Band in Tallahassee, Florida. For more than fifty years, Dr. Foster has shaped drill sessions and halftime shows. He has also molded minds of young men and women. He is indeed a legend, not only for Florida A&M University but also for this state and our nation. Dr. Foster, thank you for your many years of service. Congratulations.

BISHOP A. J. RICHARDSON

African Methodist Episcopal Church

One of the crowning successes in my life was to have been a member of the FAMU Marching "100" Band. It was a very special privilege to have been a head drum major of this world-renowned band. A part of my success as a pastor and leader in the church has resulted from the lessons learned from Dr. William P. Foster, master teacher, conductor, motivator, and psychologist.

Thank you, Doc, for all that you have meant to me. I appreciate so much your encouragement and your support through the years. Congratulations on fifty years. Hubba, Doc.

THE HONORABLE PAT THOMAS

Florida State Senator

I proudly represented FAMU in the Florida Senate for a long time. I am so proud to pay tribute to Dr. Foster. I have known him as a personal friend. He has brought great credit to our city and honor to all of us across this nation.

I think one of the more exciting days in the Senate was when he was there as my guest. He was in the Senate when they hung my portrait. As we hung that portrait, he came marching in with the Marching "100" playing "When The Saints Go Marching In." The Senate went wild. At the end of the session, senators were still asking me when Dr. Foster was coming back.

Dr. Foster is truly a legend in his own time. I am so endeared and thankful to have had a chance to know him as we passed this way.

MR. WALLACE A. CLARK

Professor of Clarinet, History of Music, and Music Education,
Florida A&M University Department of Music

Dr. Foster, it is a pleasure and an honor to render this salute commemorating your fiftieth year of service to Florida A&M University, to Tallahassee, and to the world community of musicians and music lovers. Your work awed us. It has never ceased to be thrilling, entertaining, or educating us. Your creativity is remarkable. The sheer genius in your inventiveness of presentation; your originality of ideas; your attentiveness to detail; your thoughtfulness, care, and sensitivity; your ability to inspire others—all are indeed rare among university professors. In national and international arenas, the quality of your work is exemplary.

Your consistent high level of precision and dedication to an idea are both heartwarming and instructive. I suspect that rarely have you deviated from your artistic goals; probably in a given situation you would have held the Philadelphia Orchestra to the same high standards that you have routinely exacted at Florida A&M University. You have held yourself to even higher standards. In fact, your highly polished professional and aristocratic manner is reminiscent of the admonitions of the distinguished French conductor, Jean Fournet. Clearly, your characteristic sophistication and personal bearing are symbolic of his classroom instructions to us.

Thanks to you, Dr. Foster, when I left Florida A&M University in 1961 for graduate study at Indiana University, I was well prepared for the challenges and terrors of artistic advancement. You had ensured my familiarity, comfort, and competence with exacting standards and classical renditions of music. Countless times during my years as a student at Florida A&M University, I saw you work magic in Les

Preludes and other reputable creations with the Florida A&M University Symphonic Band. I remember, even now, how you worked opening pizzicato notes with our tubas, string bass, and contrabass clarinets. The effect and affective response were sheer sorcery. You asked that every note sing. When you finished your hour, indeed, the notes did sing. While in graduate school in Italy, I was both excited and gratified to observe the late great and legendary conductor of the La Scala Opera, Franco Ferrara, "fostering" similar techniques among his students.

The similarities continue through Sergiu Celibidache, conductor of the Munich Philharmonic. He and you are the only two musicians I know who can achieve the effect of "endless melody" that Wagner asked for in the Tristan und Isolde "Liebestod" music. Your use of staggered breathing among our winds achieved the same contours as his bowings did for the strings of the Munich Philharmonic. As I watched the two of you work the same composition, the effect was amazing. Not only were your voices and styles of command very similar but also your ears for the perfectly phrased musical line and your ear for richness of sonority were nearly identical.

Today, I am happy to report that we at Florida A&M University are exceedingly proud to have you, an esteemed master, in our midst. You have shared your gifts freely with us. We could not have made this musical journey without you. We appreciate all that you have done and forever we will hold you in highest regard.

COACH COSTA KITTLES AND DR. EMMA KITTLES

Baseball Coach
Florida A&M University

As graduates of FAMU, my wife and I are very proud of Dr. Foster's outstanding contributions to our beloved alma mater. We also have great admiration for him as an accomplished and world-renowned band director.

In addition to his numerous accolades in the music world, he is also respected as a humanitarian and student advocate. I can recall his many acts of kindness and cooperation when I served as FAMU's baseball coach. There were times when I needed lime to mark off the baseball field, and he willingly gave me the key to the band's lime supply, as the band also used lime to mark off their practice field. Many times he shared his student-waiver fees for out-of-state students with me to make it possible for an impoverished out-of-state baseball player to receive an education at FAMU.

When Dr. Foster served as chairman of the student disciplinary committee, he always considered the potential of students to change their behavior and gave them a chance to do so. He was instrumental in helping many of my baseball players by putting them on probation instead of suspending them from the university. However, he was extremely fair in his decisions and would not hesitate to "crack the whip" when it became necessary.

My wife and I shall always have a place in our hearts for Dr. Foster as a leader, father figure, role model, and good friend.

MS. GLORIA JONES

Secretary to Dr. William P. Foster, 1974–1998

When I think of Dr. William P. Foster, many words come to mind: integrity, trustworthiness, loyalty, compassion, empathy, peacefulness, gentleness, and brilliance.

It was a rewarding experience for me to work as his secretary for twenty-three years. His expectations of himself and others were high. He never settled for less than the best that a person had to offer. He believes in excellence and strives for it daily. His daily standards have made him the legend that he is today.

DR. JOHN M. LONG

Dean of the School of Fine Arts, Director of Bands,
and Distinguished Professor Emeritus
Troy State University

One of the most memorable experiences of my life was when I introduced Dr. William Foster to the members of the American Band-masters Association (ABA). Bill had just been elected president of the ABA. It was a very moving time because I, along with Dr. William Revelli, another friend of Dr. Foster's, had worked a long time to get Dr. Foster elected.

Bill had done so many things for so many people, and now, he was president of the most prestigious band organization in the world, the American Bandmasters Association.

In my introduction of Dr. Foster, I told the other members of the ABA how Bill had started in Tuskegee, Alabama, and had done a great job. I told them how hard it had been for him to work his way through the University of Kansas and to earn his doctorate.

I told them about Bill's many successes. I told the American Band-masters that his success was the result of his never turning his back on any of his students. He was always there for them in every way when they needed him. He kept a firm but guiding hand on everything they did from the time they entered Florida A&M until the time they left. His students not only revered and respected him, but they also loved him because they knew he always had their best interest at heart.

Many of the students graduated at Florida A&M due to Dr. Foster's perseverance and because he insisted that they stay in school. I have seen Bill Foster reach into his pocket, hand some band members money, and say "Pay me back someday," knowing that they would not be able to pay him back any time in the near future. The real truth is that they have paid him back many times in the successes they have had because of him.

I have never seen a member of the Florida A&M band who did not love and respect this man. Dr. Foster has carried the band to places no other band has gone. I reminded the other members of the ABA of his service to the Florida Bandmasters Association and of the great success he had as president of the College Band Directors National Association (CBDNA). In fact, the CBDNA had the greatest year ever under Bill's leadership.

Introducing Bill to the ABA membership was a great moment for me. I had a chance to point out to our members that Bill was truly one of the great American living legends. I wanted our members to know that our organization would achieve new heights under his leadership—and we did. Having had the opportunity to express my true feelings for this great man was truly a great moment in my life.

MR. JOSEPH "JOE" BULLARD

The Voice of the Marching "100"

This is a celebration of "the Man" and his accomplishments. We have gathered to pay tribute to an outstanding, world-renowned leader, Dr. William P. Foster. He is better known to some as the "Maestro" and to others as "The Law."

It is fitting that we recognize and thank Dr. Foster for sharing his gifts and his enormous talents with the world. While doing so, he equally brings honor to himself and to Florida A&M University for which we say, "Thank you, Dr. Foster."

When The Maestro raises his baton, his genius is poured into his work, and his creativity produces the magic that has earned him the international reputation of "the best band director in the land." For this, Doc, we say to you, congratulations!

Dr. Foster's legendary work with the Florida A&M University Marching "100" Band is awesome. Having garnered every award imaginable, including the coveted Sudler Award and receiving an invitation from the French to represent the United States of America in the French Bastille Day Celebration in Paris, France, speaks to the kind of recognition of which others can only dream. Again, Dr. Foster, we thank you.

And so, tonight we have come together to honor Dr. William Patrick Foster. By doing so, we give testimony to a leader and a legend.

THE HONORABLE ALFRED LAWSON

Former Florida State Senator

It is a pleasure and an honor to offer a few remarks about my good friend, Dr. William P. Foster. I have known Dr. Foster personally over the past thirty years. For seventeen of those years, he has been both a neighbor and someone with whom I have shared a great deal of time reflecting on his outstanding career and his loving family.

Dr. Foster has truly made outstanding contributions to the field of music and is recognized as an outstanding Floridian. With his extraordinary leadership and remarkable talent, he has created the most outstanding band in the United States. He has received numerous accolades in America and abroad for his achievements, including having been inducted into the Hall of Fame.

On a personal note, Dr. Foster is always involved in his church and various community organizations. He is truly recognized among his peers as a person who has always been ahead of his time. He has made tremendous strides that have enhanced musical opportunities for young people. The contributions that he has made are so creative, so original, and so ingenious that they could never be replicated.

He has given over fifty years of service to the members of the

Florida Agricultural and Mechanical University family as a professor, conductor, director of bands, and the list goes on. He is one of the most sought-after persons in music by other universities for their lecture series.

I am very fortunate to have known and worked with Dr. Foster for so many years. Dr. William P. Foster is to be revered, not only as a great Floridian but as a great American hero.

DR. LEEDELL W. NEYLAND

Professor of History Emeritus, Former Dean of Arts and Sciences, and Vice President For Academic Affairs
Florida A&M University

Dr. William P. Foster stands out in my memory as one of the most scholarly, dedicated, and highly accomplished professors/administrators with whom I have ever worked.

His life and works not only exemplify excellence as a teacher, administrator, researcher, and writer of professional books and articles but also in creative, imaginative, inspirational, and entertaining musical activities, which gave rise to the world-renowned Florida A&M University Marching "100" Band.

Dr. Foster was one of a group of fifteen professors who joined the FAMC faculty in 1946, under the presidency of Dr. William H. Gray, Jr. This group was designated as the "Famous Faculty Class of 1946." For fifty-five years, Foster's outstanding achievements and contributions in the field of music have not only made him an internationally famous musical leader, but they have contributed to FAMU's image as a leading institution of higher learning on the state, national, and international levels.

Having served with Foster for more than forty years as a professional colleague, his academic dean, and his vice president for academic affairs, I have seen firsthand his academic ability as a department chairman and his versatility as a bandmaster. He has been credited with revolutionizing marching band techniques through the use of dance, general showmanship, fine music, precision marching, and a quick-stepping tempo that reached 320 steps a minute. Foster is credited with increasing band participation from sixteen members in 1946 to 329 members when he retired in 1998. As a scholar and writer, his concepts and intricate maneuvers for college bands are included in his textbook, *Band Pageantry*, which is considered by some as the bible for marching bands.

When I reflect on the most honored, most publicized, and most imitated bands in America, inevitably the FAMU Marching Band comes into focus. Evidence that Foster's band was world renowned may be seen in the facts that he has appeared on all major television networks, played at halftime shows for three Super Bowls, appeared in two inaugural parades for President Bill Clinton, and represented America with the FAMU Marching Band in Paris, France participating in the 200th Anniversary Bastille Day Parade. It was no surprise that FAMU's marching band was given the prestigious Sudler Intercollegiate Marching Band Trophy from the John Philip Sousa Foundation.

In addition to his success with the Marching "100," Foster expanded his reputation as a versatile musician and conductor through the FAMU Symphony Band, which has performed in a joint concert with the United States Army Band in Constitution Hall, Washington, D.C. and in other musical halls throughout the country.

After fifty-two years of active leadership, Foster resigned and the university bestowed upon him the title of chairman of the Department of Music and director of bands emeritus, as well as an honorary doctor of humane letters. He was also appointed the position of Eminent Scholar of the Foster-Edmond Chair. On the state level, the governor and the cabinet of the State of Florida selected Foster for inclusion in the "Great Floridian" series. Throughout Florida, many supporters call him the "Artist of the Century."

Even though Dr. Foster earned many accolades and praises for his memorable accomplishments and achievements in the field of music, he readily admits that his most lasting satisfaction comes from the thousands of students whom he has touched and inspired during his fifty-five years of service. He admits that his heart is enriched when bandleaders, who are graduates of FAMU, field bands that try to imitate the Marching "100." I am convinced that Dr. Foster has left a legacy of dedication, devotion, and superior accomplishment in the field of music and marching bands at FAMU that will never be equaled.

BERNARD W. KINSEY

Class of 1966—"A Lesson for a Lifetime"

As a freshman in August 1961, I came to FAMU with great anticipation and for one reason only: to play in the FAMU Marching "100." Everyone who played in the band has his or her favorite stories about Dr. Foster, affectionately called "The Law."

In 1963, the Marching "100" was scheduled to perform at the "NFL Championship" game in Miami, Florida, the first such appearance by a college band. Dr. Foster scheduled practice to ensure that we were perfectly prepared. I decided, along with a couple of fellow band members, that we could skip practice because we were upperclassmen. When we returned to the hotel, Dr. Foster informed us that we would be "sitting out" this performance and would not be allowed to march. The next day on the front page of the Miami Herald was an overhead color photograph of my French horn section with a vacant space ... mine!

Dr. Foster frequently taught us "life lessons"—in my case a very painful lesson that I haven't forgotten in nearly forty years. That experience made me a better person and caused me to become more disciplined, more focused, and a stickler for detail and follow-up.

Dr. Foster's teachings, leadership, and character taught countless men and women to be responsible, mature, and contributing adults.

To this day, one of the most powerful experiences in my life is to have been a part of the Marching "100." I am fortunate to have had an opportunity to grow and learn under Dr. Foster.

MR. LINDSEY B. SARJEANT

Chairman of the Department of Music, 2014-present, Florida A&M University

When I first me Dr. Foster as a student, I was pleasantly surprised at his overall professional demeanor and gentleman-style quality. He was elegant; yet, he lived up to his reputation of being "The Law." As I participated in marching and symphonic bands, I soon realized what a masterful musician he was.

He would rehearse the band, one note at a time, in order to gain perfection, and he always paid close attention to the smallest detail, both musically and professionally.

When I joined the staff as the arranger for the FAMU Marching Band, I was always amazed at Dr. Foster's musical interpretations of my arrangements. He is able to pull musical things out of my arrangements that I did not know were there. As a result, the arrangements were enhanced far beyond my expectations. The overall sound and interpretation are one of the trademarks of the FAMU Marching Band. No one, as it relates to current musical styles and trends, surpasses Dr. Foster's depth and understanding of music. In that way, he stands alone.

MR. CHARLES S. BING

Associate Director of Bands,
Florida A&M University

The year was 1955. Perhaps the month was December, when, as a high school senior, I noticed a utility post in Orlando, Florida that I will never forget. A poster sign was affixed to it, which advertised an upcoming performance in Lakeland, Florida by "The Famous 132-piece Florida A&M University Marching Band" directed by Dr. William P. Foster. I was "hooked" by the fact that the word "famous" was used to describe the FAMU Marching Band. Although I had never heard or seen the band, I wanted "to be in that number" and see firsthand what it was all about.

Within the next six months, several good things would happen in my life. Among them, I would graduate salutatorian from high school and receive a music scholarship to attend Florida A&M University.

Upon enrolling at this institution, little did I know that my life would be changed so drastically and remarkably from a standpoint of growth and musicianship.

The first person I met at my new "home away from home" was Dr. William Patrick Foster. There was something very noticeable about this man called "The Law." He was always professionally dressed, even on the band rehearsal field. His every walk was with dignity. Of great importance was the fact that we were being guided by a master who "went by the book" and was the jury, the judge, and "The Law." However, make no mistake about it—the entire band respected him. They knew that everyone would be treated fairly. For the many of us who needed a role model to serve as a powerful identifying figure, Dr. Foster, a man of impeccable character, was that all-important person.

For four years as an undergraduate student, I was very appreciative of the training that was given to me. Very vividly, I can recall Dr. Foster meticulously charting all of the formations for our band presentations. Every conceivable and minute detail for each band member to follow was recorded on the drill charts. With such practice, procedure, and organization, the band members were able to learn and perfect the formations to a degree that otherwise would have been very difficult. This same degree of perfection was always the goal of Dr. Foster, whether or not it was preparing the symphonic band for a performance on campus or for a national event.

After graduating from Florida A&M University in 1960, my life was further enhanced. Dr. Foster gave me an opportunity to teach at this great institution. For the next four decades, I was able to work and grow under the watchful eyes of a person we all called a perfectionist.

As members of the band staff, we always respected Dr. Foster for being fair to us. Never would he refuse input from us. However, by the same token, if a suggestion did not fit or would not enhance the band's performance, he would make his feelings known in a tactful yet straightforward manner. For example, many of us still employed with the band staff recall an experience when one of our talented staff members gave a demonstration of some of his ideas that featured some fancy footwork for a dance routine. Dr. Foster, without a smile, or frown, tactfully "cut" those dance routine steps down to a simple knee lift. For all practical purposes, considering time and everything else (such as precision in execution and audience appeal), Dr. Foster made the right decision.

Having worked for more years with Dr. Foster than with any other member of his band staff, I am of the opinion that his greatest administrative decisions involved hiring his own "homegrown" students to work as teachers and band staff members. This appears to be a practice that is destined to continue producing a rich and bountiful harvest. Of course, we all know that good things do end. However, thanks to the foresight and wisdom of Dr. William P. Foster, "The Law," fruitful seeds have been planted and will continue to germinate and sustain us for many years to come.

SYLVESTER YOUNG, PH.D.

Director, Florida A&M University Marching "100" 2013-2016

I owe my career and success in music education to Dr. William P. Foster. I am so excited that I have an opportunity to share some of my thoughts of Dr. William P. Foster, founder of the FAMU Marching "100." My tenure at FAMU was from 1965–1969. I was a music education major, and trombone was my primary instrument. I knew immediately that I wanted to be like Dr. Foster after I heard him speak to my freshmen class. My meeting and interacting with Dr. Foster set the standard for me of what a college professor should be. I cherished every minute I was in his presence to include meetings, advising, and all rehearsals. I can remember many of the members mimicking his speech accent and the "big words" he used in the dormitory. Little as we knew, all of us used his mannerisms in our professional lives. I even used his technique of addressing the current band now, same as he did during my student years. He demonstrated to all of the students and the staff the personality, mannerisms, and work ethics of a true professional.

I should mention that my personal relationship with Dr. Foster has played an important role in my career. I have taught music at five high schools and universities. Dr. Foster called me and had me apply for three of those positions, namely, Schofield High School (Aiken, South Carolina), Howard High School (Chattanooga, Tennessee), and Ohio University (Athens, Ohio). I was fortunate that Dr. Foster remembered me and knew how committed I was to my career.

My forty-five-year career in music has taken me all over the country at many universities and school districts. I can say without a doubt, that someone always asked me about Dr. Foster and quizzed me about him and the FAMU band program. I always felt honored to share my Foster/FAMU experiences with those people.

In closing, again, I am honored to have this opportunity to share this information and am blessed that Dr. Foster played such an important part of my career and life. The highest accomplishment in my life is humbly having Dr. Foster's job as the director of the Marching "100." As Dr. Foster always ended his letters.

DR. KAWACHI A. CLEMONS

Associate Professor of Music and Director, Institute for Research in Music and Entertainment Industry Studies and

Former Chairman of the Department of Music, Florida A&M University

Dr. William P. Foster is not only the "man behind the baton", he is also the man behind the spark that ignited the careers of many African American collegiate band directors and music educators across the United States. As a young student musician I attended the FAMU Marching '100' band camp, digesting Dr. Foster's insight and commitment to extraordinary musicianship. Twenty years later I became Chair of the FAMU Department of Music. The many students who rehearsed and performed under Dr. Foster's baton echo similar stories of success in all fields of human endeavor. The tenets of his band motto guide our lives and resonate from each of our hearts. We are his legacy!

SHELBY R. CHIPMAN, PH.D

Associate Professor of Music,

Florida A&M University Department of Music

Director of the Marching 100 and University Pep Bands, May 2016-present

Dr. William Patrick Foster is without question one of the most prolific gentlemen to have assumed the position of a band director, as well as to have served as an outstanding musician, educator, scholar, and leader. During my years as a student in the Florida A&M University Department of Music and a participant in the FAMU Marching 100, I have witnessed Dr. Foster mentor many young musicians. The myriad of life lessons that are learned in the FAMU band are revered by all, and the philosophy of the Marching "100" is garnered in the band motto:

Qualities to live by to guide our thoughts and to rule our actions/lives.

"Highest quality in Character"

"Achievement in Academics"

"Attainment in Leadership"

"Perfection in Musicianship"

"Precision in Marching"

"Dedication to Service"

Upon returning to the Florida A&M University as a faculty member, he continued to provide me with tools that helped mold my career as a music educator. I will forever be grateful to him for his wisdom, superb musicianship and score preparation.

I am certainly honored to have the pleasure of recognizing "The Law," Dr. William P. Foster, for his vision and development of high standards that the incomparable Marching "100" and symphonic band are measured by throughout the world. He was truly a giant that lived during his time, and he gave of himself when others initially told him that there was no room for African Americans to study conducting. In short, Dr. Foster was an inspiration to me, the lives of students who matriculated at FAMU and persons who he conducted and associated with in music. Thank you for rekindling his life through the republication of "The Man Behind the Baton."

Achievements and Recognitions

D
r. William P. Foster is an eminent scholar, a distinguished professor, the Department of Music chairman, and the director of bands emeritus at Florida A&M University. He is the former director of the prestigious McDonald's All-American High School band (1980–1991). He is recognized as "The Dean of America's Band Directors" and one of the most important band directors in the United States of America.

KNIGHTED BY FRANCE

On August 25, 2000, Dr. Foster was awarded the Diploma of Chevalier of the Order of Arts and Letters by Mme. Catherine Tasca, Minister of Culture and Communication of France. This award recognizes eminent artists and writers who have contributed significantly to furthering the arts in France and throughout the world. In 1989, the French chose the Florida A&M University Marching "100" Band as the featured attraction of the 200th Anniversary Bastille Day Parade in Paris, July 14, 1989.

MEMBERSHIP ON THE NATIONAL COUNCIL OF THE ARTS

Appointment to the National Council of the Arts was a most prestigious national honor for Dr. Foster. He served from mid-1996 through 1998. United States Congresswoman Carrie P. Meek, a FAMU graduate, recommended Dr. Foster to President Bill Clinton for membership. After a lengthy background check by our Federal Bureau of Investigation and an affirmative vote by the United States Congress, Dr. Foster was approved. Jane Alexander, chair of the National Endowment for the Arts, notified him of his election to the Council of the Arts.

The appointment to the council was a positive statement about his contributions to the arts. It was also an acknowledgment of the positive contributions of the Florida A&M University Department of Music to the arts. Dr. Foster was the first band director and the eighth Black American elected to this organization of 165 members during a period of thirty-seven years. He has also served two terms as a member of the State of Florida Arts Council.

LABELS BESTOWED ON FOSTER

Many labels—both affectionate and serious—have been bestowed upon Dr. Foster: The Law, The Maestro, The Legend, musical and organizational genius, national treasure, greatest band director in the country, trendsetter, pacesetter, and artist of the century.

EDUCATION

Dr. Foster was a fellow of the Rockefeller Foundation General Education Board at Teacher's College, Columbia University, 1953–1955, for doctoral studies. He earned the bachelor of music education

degree from the University of Kansas in 1941, master of arts in music degree from Wayne State University in 1950, and the doctor of education degree with a major in music from Teachers College, Columbia University in 1955.

Dr. William P. Foster, left, and
Dr. Frederick Humphries,

He received the Honorary Doctor of Humane Letters Degree in 1998 from Florida A&M University.

OTHER HONORS AND AWARDS

The Cabinet of the State of Florida and the Florida Board of Regents have recognized Dr. Foster several times for distinguished achievements. He has received numerous honors, awards, and resolutions from the Florida House of Representatives and Senate.

Dr. Foster has received a Citation of Excellence from the National Band Association, a Distinguished Service Award from the University of Kansas, an Arts Achievement Award from Wayne State University, a Meritorious Achievement Award from Florida A&M University, and the ninety-ninth United States Congress honored Dr. Foster with a full-page article in its Tuesday, February 4, 1986, "Proceedings." He is a past president of the Florida Music Educators Association, the College Band Directors National Association, and the American Bandmasters Association.

HALL OF FAME INDUCTIONS

On March 9, 2000, Dr. Foster was inducted into the Music Educators National Conference Hall of Fame, during the first general session In-Service Convention. The president of the Music Educators National Association, Ms. June M. Hinckley, presented the Hall of Fame plaque. Dr. Foster was the first Black American and the second band director to receive this recognition. He has been a member of the Music Educators National Conference for more than fifty years.

At the joint conference of the Florida Music Educators National Association and the Southern Division of the Music Educators National Association, Dr. Foster received a proclamation on January 9, 1999, at the Tampa Convention Center during the opening of the joint conference. On March 12, 1999, he received a Lifetime Achievement Award from the National Association for the Study and Performance of African American Music at the awards banquet held at the Sheraton-Premiere Hotel, Tyson's Corner, Vienna, Virginia.

Dr. Foster and the FAMU Symphonic Band

On December 17, 1998, the Board of Electors in Chicago, Illinois, elected Dr. William P. Foster to the National Band Association Hall of Fame for Distinguished Band Conductors.

The internationally famous 329-piece FAMU Marching Band, for which he created more than 200 halftime pageants, has appeared in three films, three commercials, and in numerous magazines and newspaper articles. It has appeared on *60 Minutes, 20/20* and *PM Magazine* telecasts and has performed on thirty-four nationally televised programs on all networks with a viewing audience of over five billion people.

Dr. Foster and the FAMU Symphonic Band on the steps of the US Capitol in Washington, D.C.

The FAMU Marching Band was presented the prestigious Sudler Intercollegiate Marching Band Trophy on October 26, 1985. On January 27, 1996, the FAMU Marching Band was the centerpiece of the Opening Ceremonies of the Walt Disney World Indy 200 before fifty-five thousand spectators. The ceremonies were viewed by many others on the ABC national telecast. The band was also the featured attraction at the fifteenth and twenty-fifth anniversary national telecasts of Walt Disney World in 1986 and 1996.

Dr. Foster is credited with revolutionizing marching band technique and reshaping the world's concept of the collegiate marching band. He is the driving force behind the nation's most innovative college band, the Florida A&M University internationally renowned Marching "100." He is credited with creating more than fifty innovations and first performances for marching band techniques.

According to Michael Hurd in the book *Black College Football*, "Most of what you see Black college bands doing at halftime—dancing, quickstepping, general showmanship—was originated in 1946 by Dr. William P. Foster at Florida A&M University. He presented a marching band clinic to over a thousand band directors at the Midwest International Band Clinic and the Texas Bandmasters Association."

Under the baton of Dr. Foster, the Florida A&M University Symphonic Band has presented concerts for many groups: the American Bandmasters Association, Southern and National Conferences of the College Band Directors National Association, Music Educators National Conference, and the Florida Music Educators Association. The band has also performed in a joint concert with the United States Army Band ("Pershing's Own") in Constitution Hall, Washington, D.C.

Dr. Foster has served as guest conductor for numerous bands: the United States Air Force, Army, Marine, and Navy Bands, Interlochen Arts Academy Band, New York All-State Band, Michigan All-State Band, Midwest Music and Art Camp, Indiana University Symphonic Band, Nebraska All-State Band, McDonald All-American High School Band, and the Northshore Concert Band. He also guest conducted for the Kappa Kappa Psi/Tau Beta Sigma 1985 Intercollegiate Band Convention held at the University of Kansas, Lawrence, Kansas, and for the United States Interservice Band at Constitution Hall, Washington, D.C. 1992 ABA Convention.

Dr. Foster has also conducted at Carnegie Hall in New York;

Orchestra Hall in Chicago; Constitution Hall in Washington, D.C.; Jordan Hall, New England Conservatory of Music; Interlochen Bowl; National Music Camp; Music Hall in Kansas City; Brooklyn Academy of Music; the Midwest International Band and Orchestra Clinic in Chicago; and the Kennedy Center in New York.

Dr. Foster has written eighteen articles for professional journals and for marching band shows. He has written a textbook, *Band Pageantry*, which is considered as "the bible" for the marching band. He has presented clinics at more than twenty festivals and competitions ranging from state fairs to international festivals in Canada, Mexico, and Jamaica. As a visiting lecturer, he has lectured at symposia and colloquia at colleges and universities in fourteen different states. As an active professional, Dr. Foster belongs to eighteen professional organizations and ten boards and councils. He is credited with the presentation at the first National Marching-Band Clinic telecast on January 22, 1989, over the Ti-In Network.

A member of ASCAP and AFTRA, Dr. Foster is the composer of "Marche Brillante," "National Honors March," "March Continental," and "Centennial Celebration."

In 1973, the University of Kansas and its Alumni Association conferred the "Citation for Distinguished Service" upon Dr. William P. Foster. He is the first recipient of the United States Achievement Academy Hall of Fame Award and the first Outstanding Educator Award by the School of Education Society of the University of Kansas Alumni Association.

Dr. Foster was featured in a publication of the Smithsonian Institution for his developmental techniques, concepts, and philosophy on band pageantry and the role of the marching band in the school band movement for the Afro-American Conference at the Smithsonian Institute in Washington, D.C.

The Florida A&M University 1999 Homecoming of the Century Committee selected Dr. William P. Foster as one of the "100" Most Influential FAMUans of the Century. This award is in recognition of Dr. Foster's remarkable contributions to public service and education that have brought honor and distinction to Florida A&M University.

Dr. Foster is the recipient of the 2000 Lifetime Leadership Award from the Tallahassee Area Chamber of Commerce. The award was presented at the Sixth Annual Distinguished Leadership Awards Dinner held on September 21, 2000, at the University Center Club at Florida State University.

Awards

1. February 27, 1952, Spearman Brewing Company, Spearman, Brewing Company Achievement Award

2. 1965, FAMU SGA, Teacher of the Year 1964–65

3. September 25, 1971, Kansas University Alumni Association, Alumni Achievement Award

4. June 4, 1972, FAMU Student Affairs, Meritorious Award

5. October 27, 1973, University of Arizona, Milton B. Nunamaker Distinguished Director's Award

6. 1981, University of Kansas School of Education Alumni Society, First Outstanding Educator Award

7. 1982, FAMU Booster Club, Inc., Award of Excellence for Thirty-Six Years of Service

8. 1982, FAMU 1982 Ebony Fashion Fair Committee, Distinguished Service Award

9. 1983, Gamma Mu Lamda Chapter of Alpha Phi Alpha Fraternity, Inc., Silver Jubilee Award

10. December 17, 1984, John Philip Sousa Foundation, Announcement Letter: Recipient of Sudler Intercollegiate Marching-Band Trophy 1985

11. August 24, 1985, St. Michael and All Angels Episcopal Church, Community Leader Recognition Award

12. October 26, 1985, John Philip Sousa Foundation, The Sudler Trophy

13. December 8, 1985, Gamma Mu Lambda Chapter of Alpha Phi Alpha Fraternity, Inc., Outstanding Achievement Award 1985

14. November 28, 1986, City of Chicago, Mayor Harold Washington: Key to the City

15. 1986, The Rotary Foundation, Paul Harrison Fellow Award

16. October 2, 1987, Florida A&M University, Centennial Medallion

17. December 15, 1987, Wayne State University, Distinguished Alumni Award

18. March 12, 1988, Tallahassee National Achievement Award

19. June 19, 1988, City of Thomasville, Key to the City of Thomasville

20. April 23, 1989, FAMU SGA, Rattler Pride of the Year Award

21. July 14, 1989, FAMU National Alumni Association, Distinguished Service Award/Bastille Day

22. May 16, 1990, Teacher's College, Columbia University, Distinguished Alumni Award

23. June 2, 1990, Gamma Mu Lambda Chapter of Alpha Phi Alpha Fraternity, Inc., Special Achievement Award (Fifty Years of Service)

24. April 23, 1992, FAMU Concert Choir, Service Award

25. May 5, 1993, FAMU Concert Choir, Service Award

26. August 7, 1995, FAMU National Alumni Association, Miami-Dade Chapter, Distinguished Service Award (Fifty Years of Service)

27. April 25, 1996, FAMU National Alumni, Lifetime Achievement Award

28. December 1, 1996, Alpha Phi Alpha, Gamma Mu Lambda Chapter, Outstanding Alpha Man Award

29. 1997, Tallahassee Area Chapter 100 Black Men of America, Inc., Living Legend Award

30. November 15, 1997, Omega Psi Phi Fraternity, Inc., Chi Omega Chapter, Citizen of the Year Award

31. January 17, 1998, FAMU Marching "100" / PVR Video Production, Distinguished Service Award

32. February 6, 1998, National Band Association, Hall of Fame Award for Distinguished Band Conductors

33. April 8, 1998, Museum of Florida History, Great Floridian Award

34. September 17, 1998, Leadership Tallahassee, Distinguished Leadership Award

35. March 12, 1999, National Association for the Study and Performance of African American Music, Lifetime Achievement Award

36. May 16, 1999, Teachers College, Columbia University, Teachers College Distinguished Alumni Award

37. October 29, 1999, FAMU Homecoming of the Century Committee, "100" Most Influential FAMUans of the Century

38. October 29, 1999, FAMU, Millennium Award, FAMUan of the Century

39. March 8, 2000, Music Educators National Conference, MENC Hall of Fame Induction Award

40. May 25, 2000, French Minister of Culture and Communication of France, The Diploma of Chevalier of the Order of Arts and Letters

41. September 7, 2000, Leadership Tallahassee, Chamber of Commerce, Lifetime Leadership Award

42. September 14, 2000, The Hadley Family, President's Arts Achievement Award, Wayne State University

Certificates

1. April 29, 1965, Phi Mu Alpha Sinfonia Fraternity of America, Certificate of Life Paid Alumni Member

2. 1969, NCAA, Commemorative Certificate, College Football Centennial Award (1869–1969)

3. June 16–27, 1969, International Education Association, Certificate of Appreciation in Educational Workshop

4. 1970, Personalities of the South, Certification to appear in the 1970 Edition of Personalities of the South in recognition of your achievements and services

5. September 1, 1970, *The School Musician* Magazine Certificate for Most Outstanding Music Director in USA (Aug./Sept. issue)

6. June 1, 1977, Music Educators National Conference Certificate of Excellence to FAMU Symphonic Band for participation in MENC Southern Division In-Service Conference, 04/27–30/77 in Atlanta, GA

7. December 6, 1978, Leon County Sheriff Department, Certificate of Recognition

8. February 24, 1979, US Army Band and Chorus, Certificate of Achievement

9. June 8, 1979, State of Florida, Department of State Certificate of Recognition in honor of contributions to Florida's cultural atmosphere

10. January 28, 1980, Orange Bowl Committee, Certificate of Appreciation

11. May 27, 1981, Florida State of the Arts, Certificate of Recognition on being named a member of the Florida Fine Arts Council

12. 1984, McDonald's All-American High School Band Distinguished Service Certificate (11/83–01/84)

13. May 15, 1985, FAMU, Certificate of Appreciation in Music

14. 1986, Wayne State University Board of Governors, President, Faculty, Staff and Students, Certificate of Appreciation as a member of The Century Society

15. March 1, 1986, FAMU Department of Military Science/ ROTC Certificate of Appreciation

16. August 15, 1989, Duval County Public Schools, Jacksonville, Certificate of Appreciation

17. April 9, 1990, Music Educators National Conference, Certificate of Excellence

18. June 30, 1992, FAMU National Alumni Association, Tallahassee, Florida, Lifetime Membership Certificate

19. September 7, 1995, City of Miami, Certificate of Appreciation

20. September 8, 1995, Board of County Commissioners, Dade County, Certification of William P. Foster Day

21. October 12, 1995, Music Educators National Conference Certificate of Recognition for Fifty Years of Service

22. November 1, 1996, County of Los Angeles, Certificate of Congratulations

23. July 27, 1998, Florida Governor Lawton Chiles, "Florida's Finest" Certificate of Appreciation

24. August 10, 1998, Florida State University, "Your Voice TV Talk Show"

25. April 9, 2000, FAMU Collegiate Music Educators National Conference Chapter Certificate of Appreciation

26. September 6, 2000, Alpha Phi Alpha Fraternity, Inc., Fifty-Year Membership Certificate

27. October 28, 2000, Phi Beta Mu International School Bandmaster Fraternity, Honorary Member Certificate

28. 1986 FAMU Faculty Senate Certificate of Recognition for Forty Years of Service

29. John Philip Sousa Memorial Foundation, Certificate of Recognition for the Performing Arts, Washington, D.C., (John F. Kennedy Center)

Citations

1. December 18, 1959, FAMU President George W. Gore, Jr., "Grateful Recognition of Leadership of 142-Piece Marching Band"

2. January 10, 1969, City of Tallahassee, Mayor Gene Berkowitz, "Commendation for Greatest Half-Time Show"

3. May 1973, University of Kansas, Lawrence, "Distinguished Service"

4. May 21, 1978, University of Kansas Alumni Association, "Distinguished Service"

5. December 1, 1979, FAMU Alumni Association Miami Chapter, "Citation of Merit"

6. August 7, 1998, Florida State Board of Regents and FAMU, "Honorary Doctor of Humane Letters"

Honors/Tributes/ Recognitions

1. 1960, Florida State Music Educators Association, For Outstanding Service

2. September 1961, G. LeBlanc Corporation, Kenosha, WI, Elected Member of the LeBlanc Music Educators' National Advisory Board

3. 1962, Walter Mills, English White, Julian White (Drum Majors), Appreciation for your guidance and instruction, 1961–1962

4. December 8, 1962, The 1962 FAMU Marching "100," Congratulations on Diamond Anniversary, Orange Blossom Classic

5. March 2, 1966, FAMU ROTC Corps of Cadets, Salutes William P. Foster for his support of the ROTC Band

6. June 18, 1966, Florida State Music Educators Association, Appreciation for Service to the Annual FSMEA Clinic in Tallahassee (1955–1965)

7. October 10, 1969, FAMU, Dedication of Foster-Tanner Fine-Arts Center

8. August 1, 1973, The University of Michigan, Spectacular Performance as Conductor of All-State High School Band

9. February 17, 1974, US Air Force Band, Washington, D.C., Constitution Hall, Sincere Appreciation

10. 1975, FAMU Marching Band, Recognition of outstanding service to FAMU bands 1946–1975

11. February 27–March 2, 1975, Northeast Band Festival, Bermuda, Much Appreciation

12. 1976, FAMU Band, Outstanding Service to the Marching "100" Band 1976

13. February 23, 1976, LeBlanc, Kenosha, WI, Letter for Appreciation of Service

14. November 5, 1976, FAMU Band Alumni Association, In Appreciation

15. November 5, 1976, FAMU Band, Faculty and Staff, Dedication of Service

16. November 5, 1976, Brothers of Kappa Kappa Psi Delta Iota Chapter, Recognition of Meritorious Service

17. November 6, 1976, FAMU Alumni Band Reception, Tribute to Dr. William P. Foster

18. 1977, Alfred L. Watkins, For Three Decades, The Allegorical Genius Behind FAMU Bands

19. March 3, 1977, Beta Beta Lambda Chapter of Alpha Phi Alpha, Miami, Extraordinary Leadership of the Marching "100"

20. November 27, 1977, Frontiers, Appreciation for Public Service and Musical Performance

21. December 12, 1977, FAMU Band, Appreciation for Outstanding Service and Leadership to Marching Band

22. December 12, 1977, FAMU Band Staff, Outstanding Dedication and Leadership

23. 1978, Southern University Marching Band, Appreciation for Meritorious Service in the Field of Educational and Instrumental

24. December 6, 1978, FAMU Marching Band and Staff, Appreciation of Thirty-three Years of Service as Director of Bands

25. December 6, 1978, Gamma Mu Lambda Chapter of Alpha Phi Alpha Fraternity, Distinguished contributions of thirty-two years in band pageantry

26. December 6, 1978, Tallahassee Bandmasters Association, Outstanding Service to the University and City of Tallahassee

27. December 6, 1978, FAMU Concert Choir/Vernon L. Smith, "Our Best Wishes to You"

28. January 6, 1979, Miller Brewing Company, Participation in the Mighty Battle of the Bands

29. June 8, 1979, State of Florida, Secretary of State George Firestone, Letter of Appointment as Assistant to the Secretary of State for Cultural Affairs

30. December 2, 1979, University of Nevada, Appreciation for Judging Finals of the Singerland/Louie Bellson National Drum Contest

31. 1980, The National Black Music Caucus, Inspirational Leadership

32. 1981, FAMU Marching "100" Band, Outstanding dedication to Marching "100 Band, 1981

33. April 2, 1981, City of Hialeah and Hialeah Arts Board, Guest Conductor for City's Honors Band

34. May 18, 1981, Kansas University School of Education Society, Congratulations

35. 1982, FAMU Centennial Executive Associates' Club, Appreciation

36. 1982, FAMU Marching Band, Appreciation for Outstanding Service

37. May 20, 1982, Marcus Young, Director of Bands, William M. Raines Band, Parents' Achievements in Music

38. 1983, FAMU Marching Band, Outstanding Service to the Success of the Marching Band

39. January 1983, McDonald's All-American High School Band, Pasadena Tournament of Roses, Appreciation

40. September 1983, Yamaha International Corporation McDonald's All-American High School Band, Appreciation for Your Contribution to the Promotion of School Music

41. 1984, FAMU, Outstanding Service

42. 1984, Lambda Omicron Omega Chapter of Alpha Kappa Alpha Sorority, Inc., Outstanding Participating in Sarasota, 1984

43. February 25, 1984, The Clarks and Sarasota High School, Appreciation for Dr. William P. Foster

44. May 9, 1984, Atlanta Chapter FAMU Alumni Association, Appreciation of Distinguished Leadership in Music

45. 1985, Florida Music Educators Association Hall of Fame, Outstanding Contributions

46. 1985, McDonald's All-American High School Band, Appreciation of Service

47. 1985, FAMU ROTC Cadets, Forty Years of Music Perfection, 1945–1985

48. 1985, FAMU Marching Band, For Outstanding Service

49. March 14, 1985, Xerox Systems Group, Vice President. Bernard Kinsey, Letter of Congratulation for Receiving Sudler Trophy 1984

50. April 5, 1985, Dothan Alumni Chapter of Delta Sigma Theta Sorority, Appreciation for Your Contributions

51. May 1, 1985, Kappa Kappa Psi: Honorary Member, Life Membership

52. May 15, 1985, FAMU Band and Staff, Recognition for Forty Years of Service

53. August 1985, Dr. F. Lee Bowling, Kappa Kappa Psi/Tau Beta Sigma, University of Kansas, Token of Appreciation for Guest Conductor for National Intercollegiate Bands

54. September 27, 1985, FAMU Sports Hall of Fame, Appreciation for Being a Supporter

55. October 1, 1985, McDonald's, Battle of the Bands, Circle City Classic, Outstanding Participation

56. October 26, 1985, FAMU Band Staff, In Recognition of Forty Years

57. October 26, 1985, Jacksonville Chapter of the FAMU Marching "100" Band Boosters, Outstanding Leadership

58. October 26, 1985, FAMU Jazz Band, Grateful Appreciation

59. October 26, 1985, FAMU Band Student Officers, Recognition of Forty Years of Service

60. October 26, 1985, Sudler Award Recipient

61. October 27, 1985, FAMU Percussion Ensemble Honors William P. Foster as Director of Bands for Forty Years

62. 1986, FAMU Centennial Executive Associates' Club, Appreciation and Support

63. January 1, 1986, McDonald's All-American High School Band, Pasadena Tournament of Roses, Appreciation

64. February 16, 1986, The Men of the Alpha Xi Chapter of Kappa Alpha Psi Salutes William P. Foster, Outstanding Black Educator

65. September 4, 1986, United States House of Representatives, Honorable Don Fuqua of Florida, *Congressional Record*, 1986 Proceedings, Vol. 132, #9

66. October 11, 1986, McDonald's, Battle of the Bands, In Appreciation for Your Participation in Indianapolis

67. 1987, FAMU Marching Band, Outstanding Service as Director of Bands, 1986–1987

68. July 7, 1987, FAMU Band and Staff, Recognition of Forty-two Years of Service

69. July 7, 1987, FAMU Alumni, Kansas City Area Board of Directors, William P. Foster "The Conductors' Conductor

70. July 7, 1987, Herman Joseph, A Brand of Adolph Coors Company, Kansas and Missouri Distributors, A Salute to the Man Behind the Baton

71. November 14, 1987, FAMU Band, Recognition of Forty-Two Years of Dedicated Service

72. November 14, 1987, FAMU Student Government Association, Forty-Two Years of Service

73. 1988, FAMU Marching Band Honors William P. Foster for Outstanding Service, 1987–1988

74. May 27, 1988, Risley Middle School Band, Brunswick, GA, Outstanding Service

75. November 26, 1988, Bethune-Cookman College, Academic Excellence in Performing Arts

76. November 26, 1988, FAMU Band & Bethune Cookman Band, Special Tribute to William P. Foster

77. 1989, McDonald's All-American High School Band Pasadena Tournament of Roses, Recognition and Appreciation for Musical Entrants

78. 1989, FAMU Marching Band Honors William P. Foster for Outstanding Service 1988–1989

79. 1989, FAMU Student Government Association, Welcome Back From Paris – Congratulations

80. March 1, 1989, FAMU Symphonic Band, Appreciation for Outstanding Service, Fifty-fifth Annual Convention of American Bandmasters Association

81. March 19, 1989, Deerfield Park Performing Arts, Magnet School, Deerfield Beach., FL , Congratulations on Your Participation in Bastille Day Parade, Paris, France

82. June 14, 1989, WIQI Radio, Chicago, Appreciation for Representing the USA in the Bicentennial Bastille Day Parade, Paris France

83. July 1989, FAMU Industry Cluster Salutes William P. Foster and Marching "100" for Their Performance in Bicentennial Bastille Day Parade in Paris, France

84. July 1989, Tampa Chapter of the FAMU Alumni Association Salutes William P. Foster for Participation in the French Bicentennial Bastille Day Parade, Paris, France

85. July 17, 1989, United States Senate *Congressional Record,* Vol. 135 - #95

86. July 18, 1989, City of Tallahassee, Mayor Dorothy Inman Salutes Marching "100" on Performance in Bastille Day Parade in Paris, France

87. July 18, 1989, United States House of Representatives, Honorable Bill Grant of Florida, *Congressional Record,* Vol. 135 - #96

88. August 4, 1989, United States House of Representatives, Honorable Edolphus Towns of New York, *Congressional Record,* Vol. 135, #109

89. August 4, 1989, United States House of Representatives, Honorable William H. Gray, III of Pennsylvania, *Congressional Record,* Vol. 135, #109

90. October 1989, Miami-Dade Community College, Wolfson Campus, Special Recognition for Contributions to the Hispanic-Heritage 1989 Celebration

91. December 12, 1989, Bethel A.M.E. 124th Church Anniversary, Special Recognition Poem "Dr. Foster's Band" by Anthony Y. Roberts

92. 1990, Atlanta Classic 1990, Appreciation for Outstanding Performance

93. 1990, Tallahassee Urban League, Inc., Century Member

94. January 11, 1990, Florida Music Educators Association Black Caucus Forty-sixth Annual FMEA Conference, Tampa, In Appreciation

95. June 1, 1990, Tallahassee Chapter, The Links, Inc., Recognition of Notable Achievements in Music

96. November 17, 1990, People of the Bahamas, Nassau, Distinguished Professor

97. 1991, The University of Kansas Gold Medal Club Welcomes William P. Foster into Membership

98. 1991, FAMU Marching "100", Outstanding Service as Director of Bands 1990–91

99. July 1991, Northern Central Region FAMU Alumni Association, Outstanding Achievement

100. November 8, 1991, FAMU Publishers of The Classic Times Communications, Inc., On the Right Track Salutes William P. Foster

101. 1992, Miami Center High School Band, For Your Elegant Words and Sharing of Music with Us and the World, 1991–1992

102. February 15, 1992, GMEA/District II Symphonic Band Clinician, Outstanding Service

103. April 10, 1992, Four Seasons Xia Community Production Commitment to Youth Arts, Music Education, and the Community

104. April 10, 1992, FAMU President Frederick Humphries, Recognition of Appreciation for Forty-two Years of Outstanding Service

105. August 30, 1992, Elizabeth Popular Spring Primitive Baptist Church Scholarship Foundation, Appreciation for Your Valuable Service to the Youth and Community

106. October 31, 1992, FAMU Band Alumni, Homecoming Band Alumni Reunion, Outstanding Leadership

107. December 5, 1992, Beta Phi Chapter of Tau Beta Sigma Sorority, for Your Support and Care

108. January 8, 1993, Florida Music Educators Association Black Caucus, Recognition and Appreciation for Leadership in Organizing The Florida State Music Teachers Association, Tampa, FL

109. November 6, 1993, FAMU Band Alumni, Homecoming Band Alumni Reunion, Outstanding Leadership

110. October 1, 1993, FAMU National Alumni Association, Recognition of Outstanding Contribution and Service

111. April 24, 1994, FAMU, Outstanding Service to Marching "100"

112. November 12, 1994, City of Riviera Beach, FL, Appreciation for Commitment to the Community

113. January 21, 1995, FAMU Marching "100"—Outstanding Service as Director of Bands

114. 1995, FAMU Junior Class, Appreciation for Outstanding Service to FAMU

115. 1995, WPOM—Thanks for being a stepping stone in preparing great minds for the future.

116. May 4, 1995, President Bill Clinton, Thank You Letter for All Your Help During My Visit to Tallahassee

117. December 3, 1995, Miami Central Senior High School Band Honors William P. Foster for His Commitment and Dedication to Music Education

118. March 3, 1996, FAMU, Third Annual President's Concert, Golden Anniversary as Director of Bands

119. May 19, 1996, Patrice Minor-Floyd, Director of North Florida String Institute, Tallahassee, FL, For Giving Us Our Start in the Classroom-Teaching Experience

120. July 27, 1996, The Afro-American Hall of Fame, Inc., Recognition for Outstanding Achievements

121. October 5, 1996, McDonald's All-American High School Band, Coca-Cola Circle City Classic, Outstanding Participation in Battle of the Band, RCA Dome

122. October 15, 1996, McDonald's of Central Indiana, McDonald's All-American High School Band, Special Recognition for Service

123. October 29, 1996, Busch Gardens, Joseph Fincher, Executive Vice President and General Manager, Fiftieth Anniversary

124. November 1, 1996, FAMU Jazz Band, Fifty Years of Service to the Department of Music

125. November 1, 1996, FAMU STRIKERS, Fifty Years of Leadership, Service and Dedication

126. November 1, 1996, FAMU Symphony No. 50, Fifty Years of Outstanding Service

127. November 1, 1996, FAMU President Frederick Humphries, Fifty Years of Service

128. November 1, 1996, FAMU Bands, Fifty Years of Outstanding Leadership as Director of Bands

129. November 1, 1996, FAMU Marching "100" Band Staff, Fifty Years of Outstanding Service

130. November 1, 1996, FAMU College of Arts and Sciences Salutes Director of Bands on Golden Anniversary

131. November 1, 1996, FAMU Department of Music, In Appreciation of Fifty Years of Service

132. November 19, 1996, FAMU Faculty Senate, Fifty Years of Service

133. December 7, 1996, FAMU Marching "100", Fifty Golden Years of Outstanding Service

134. December 7, 1996, FAMU Flute Choir Salutes William P. Foster on Golden Anniversary

135. December 7, 1996, FAMU Percussion Ensemble Salutes William P. Foster on Fifty Years of Musicianship

136. December 7, 1996, Beta Phi Chapter of Tau Beta Sigma National Honorary Band Sorority, Appreciation for FAMU

137. April 22, 1997, FAMU President Frederick Humphries, Fifty Years of Outstanding Service

138. November 15, 1997, South Carolina State University Bands, Appreciation for "Setting the Standard of Excellence" for All Marching Bands in the World

139. January 9, 1998, Bethune-Cookman College Department of Music Celebrates William P. Foster and his contribution to music education

140. January 17, 1998, FAMU Marching "100", Outstanding Service as Director of Bands

141. March 10, 1998, Governor Paul E. Patton, Kentucky, Commissioned as a Kentucky Colonel

142. April 3, 1998, The Florida Conference of Black State Legislators - "Great Floridian"

143. April 3, 1998, FAMU Marching "100" Band, In Honor of Being A "Great Floridian"

144. April 4, 1998, Seventh District Omega Psi Phi Fraternity, Inc., Citizen of the Year, 1998

145. April 25, 1998, FAMU Choral Division, Appreciation for your contribution and service

146. August 7, 1998, Florida Board of Regents – Doctor of Humane Letters

147. August 28, 1998, Miami Central High School Band Family, Outstanding Service to Music Educators and the State of Florida

148. September 2, 1998, United States Senate *Congressional Record*, Tribute to William P. Foster and Marching "100" Band

149. September 8, 1998,United States Senator Bob Graham, Senatorial Recognition of Retirement

150. November 26, 1998, Bernard K. Jackson, Florida Classic, Appreciation for "Saint Patrick" Florida Representative Chris Smith, Ft. Lauderdale, Congratulations on Fifty-two Years

151. 1999, Andrew Buggs, Sr. and the late Marie Buggs, Appreciation for Service to Our Six Children

152. January 8, 1999, Florida Music Educators Association Black Caucus, Retirement after Fifty-two Years of Service

153. February 6, 1999, The National Hall of Fame of Distinguished Band Conductors, Hawkins-Long Hall of Honor, Troy State University

154. February 24, 1999, Xerox Corporation, Congratulations on Fifty-two Years of Outstanding Service

155. March 19, 1999, Broward County Alumni Chapter of FAMU Second Annual Scholarship Banquet, Appreciation

156. August 8, 1999, The United States Army Band, Washington, D.C., Honorary Member of Army Band

157. February 20, 2000, St. Michael and All Angels Church, Dedicated Service

158. March 2000, Music Educators National Conference, Inductee to The Music Educators Hall of Fame

159. April 22, 2001, FAMU Department of Music, A Cabaret, Concert and Reception in Appreciation of Service and Support

Proclamations

1. March 15, 1966, City of Kansas City, KS, Honorary Citizen of the City of Kansas City

2. December 7, 1974, Mayor Maurice Ferre, Miami, "William P. Foster Day"

3. March 13, 1975, Florida Governor Rueben Askew, "Music in our Schools Day"

4. April 30, 1977, Mayor Maynard Jackson, Atlanta, "William P. Foster and FAMU Band Day"

5. February 24, 1979, The District of Columbia, Washington, D.C., "FAMU Band Day"

6. November 25, 1983, City of Providence, Mayor Vincent A. Cianci, Jr., "McDonald's All-American High School Band Day"

7. November 26, 1983, The Commonwealth of Massachusetts, Gov. Michael Dukakis, "McDonald's All-American High School Band Day"

8. May 15, 1985, Mayor Hurley Rudd, Tallahassee, For Outstanding Contributions to Tallahassee, FAMU, and the Community

9. September 8, 1985, Broward County Commissioners, "William P. Foster Day"

10. September 27, 1985, City of Tallahassee, "FAMU Sports Hall of Fame Induction Ceremony Day"

11. July 7, 1987, Jackson County Executives, Kansas City, KS, Salutes Dr. William P. Foster

12. July 7, 1987, Gov. Mike Hayden, State of Kansas, "William P. Foster Day"

13. July 7, 1987, Mayor Richard Berkeley, Kansas City, MO, "William P. Foster Day"

14. July 7, 1987, Board of County Commissioners, Wyandotte County, Kansas, "William P. Foster Day"

15. July 7, 1987, Honorable Bill Waris, Jackson County, Missouri, Office of the Executive

16. March 12, 1988, Governor Bob Martinez, Florida, "William P. Foster Day"

17. March 12, 1988, Mayor Frank Visconti, Tallahassee, FL, "William P. Foster Day"

18. July 4–14, 1989, Mayor Dot Inman, Tallahassee, "FAMU Marching "100" Week

19. July 18, 1989, Board of Leon County Commissioners, "Marching "100" Month"

20. September 27, 1989, Governor of the State of Georgia, Joe Frank Harris, Congratulations to FAMU Marching Band for Outstanding Achievements

21. December 10, 1989, Flipper Chapel AME Church Board, "FAMU Marching "100" Day at Flipper Chapel"

22. May 15, 1992, Mayor Paul Keenan, Albany, GA, For Outstanding Accomplishments

23. September 22, 1996, City of Charleston, "William P. Foster Day"

24. September 4, 1998, City of Tallahassee, Mayor Scott Maddox, "Dr. William P. Foster Day"

25. September 4, 1998, Governor Lawton Chiles, Florida, "William P. Foster Day"

26. January 8, 1999, Music Educators National Conference, Fifty-Two Years of Outstanding Service

27. February 3, 1999, Broward County Board of County Commissioners, Appreciation and Recognition Banquet for Lifetime of Service

Resolutions

1. January 14, 1969, State of Florida and Leon County, Outstanding Performance in Super Bowl Professional Football Game, Orange Bowl in Miami, FL, and Gator Bowl in Jacksonville, FL

2. January 14, 1969, Paul Hartsfield, Clerk of the Circuit Court, "Commendation"

3. June 1, 1977, Florida House of Representatives (#2375), "Commendation"

4. May 15, 1985, Florida Representative Al Lawson, House of Representatives (#1384), "Commendation"

5. May 15, 1985, Florida Secretary of State George Firestone, "Commendation"

6. May 15, 1985, Florida Board of County Commissioners, "William P. Foster Day"

7. May 16, 1985, Florida Senate (#1245), "Commendation"

8. November 5, 1985, State of Florida, Governor Bob Graham, "Sudler and John Philip Sousa Foundation"

9. November 5, 1985, State of Florida, Governor Bob Graham, "Marching 100 & William P. Foster Day"

10. March 27, 1986, Florida Board of Regents, "Commendation"

11. November 3, 1987, State of Florida, "Gratitude for National Exposure and Prominence in Celebrity Centennial

12. May 27, 1988, Mayor and City Council of Brunswick, GA, "Appreciation for Your Interest in the Risley Middle School Band"

13. May 30, 1989, State of Florida House of Representatives (#1834), Commendation for Bastille Day Parade in Paris, France

14. June 2, 1989, Florida Senators Thomas and Meek (#1574), "Commendation for Bastille Day Parade in Paris, France"

15. June 27, 1989, Board of Leon County Commissioners, "Marching '100' Month"

16. July 19, 1989, FSU Forty-first Student Senate, Commendation for Dr. Foster and Marching "100"

17. September 15, 1989, House of Representatives, "Commendation"

18. November 3, 1989, Governor Bob Martinez, Commendation for Bastille Day Parade in Paris, France

19. January 26, 1990, City of Los Angeles, "Commendation"

20. February 24, 1990, California Legislature Assembly, Resolution #450, "Commendation"

21. February 24, 1990, County of Los Angeles, "Commendation"

22. November 8, 1994, FAMU Student Senate, Senate Resolution SR94F-006, "Band Appreciation Day"

23. April 17, 1996, The Florida Senate,Senators Thomas and Holzendorf, "Commendation"

24. October 28, 1996, FAMU Student Senate, Resolution SR96F-007, "Salutes W.P.F. and Marching "100"

25. March 24, 1998, Florida Governor Lawton Chiles and Cabinet of the State, "Great Floridian"

26. January 8, 1999, Florida Music Educators Association: "Outstanding Career and Many Contributions to Music Education"

27. September 4, 1998, Board of County Commissioners, Leon County, "Outstanding Achievement"

THE FLORIDA A&M UNIVERSITY
MARCHING "100" BAND

DR. WILLIAM PATRICK FOSTER'S FAMILY TREE

FATHER'S FAMILY TREE

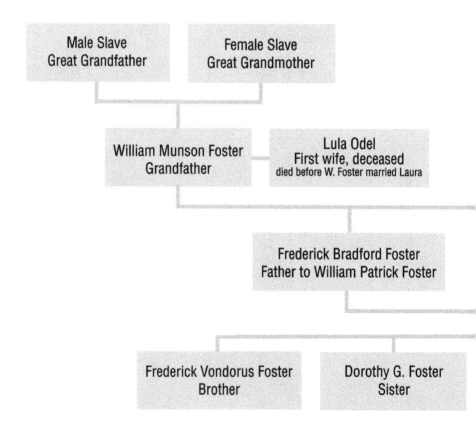

| Slave Master Great Great Grandfather | Female Slave Great Great Grandmother |

| "Undertaker" Ransom Great Grandfather | Ann Ransom "Grannie Ransom" Great Grandmother |

Laura Ann Ransom
Grandmother

See Mother's Family Tree

Venetia Highwarden-Foster
Mother to
William Patrick Foster

| Delphos Leroy Foster Brother | William Patrick Foster *The Man Behind The Baton* |

See William P. Foster Family Tree

DR. WILLIAM PATRICK FOSTER'S
FAMILY TREE

MOTHER'S FAMILY TREE

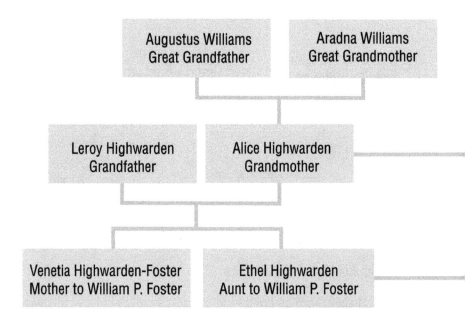

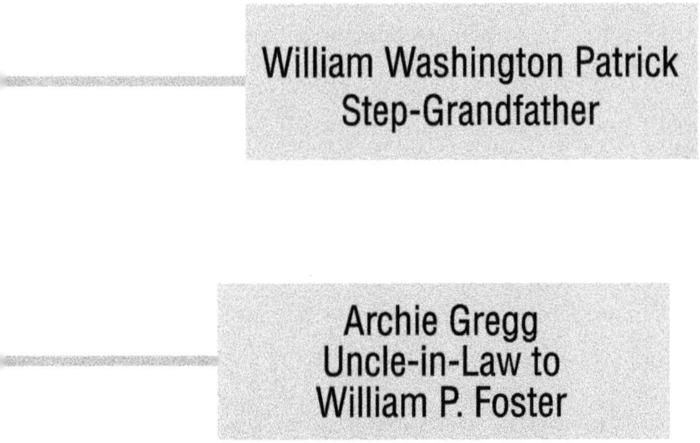

William Washington Patrick
Step-Grandfather

Archie Gregg
Uncle-in-Law to
William P. Foster

DR. WILLIAM PATRICK FOSTER'S FAMILY TREE

THE FAMILY OF DR. WILLIAM PATRICK FOSTER

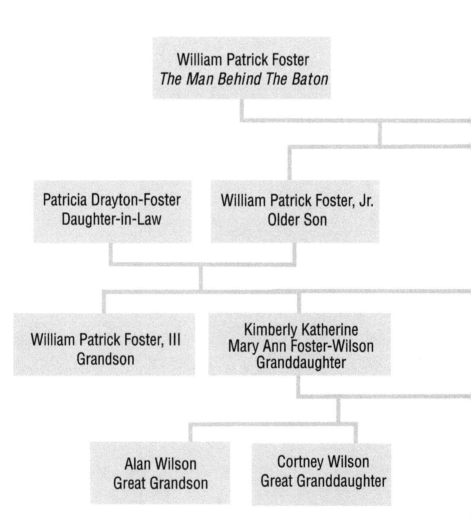

William Patrick Foster
The Man Behind The Baton

Patricia Drayton-Foster
Daughter-in-Law

William Patrick Foster, Jr.
Older Son

William Patrick Foster, III
Grandson

Kimberly Katherine
Mary Ann Foster-Wilson
Granddaughter

Alan Wilson
Great Grandson

Cortney Wilson
Great Granddaughter

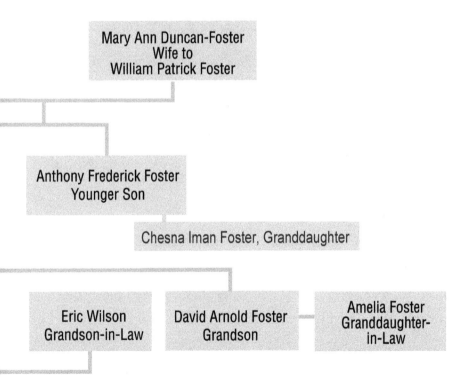

BIBLIOGRAPHY

Neyland, Leedell W. and John W. Riley, *The History of Florida Agricultural and Mechanical University* (Gainesville, Florida: University of Florida Press, 1963).

Foster, William Patrick, *Band Pageantry; A Guide for the Marching Band* (Winona, Minnesota: Hal Leonard Music, Inc., 1968).

Hall, David, *William P. Foster—American Music Educator: A Thesis submitted to the School of Music* (Tallahassee, Florida: Florida State University Department of Music, Spring, 1989).

Gordon, Jacob U., *Narratives of African Americans in Kansas, 1870–1992: Beyond the Exodust Movement* (Lewiston, New York: Edwin Meller Press, Ltd. 1993).

Malone, Jacqui, *Steppin' on the Blues: The Visible Rhythms of African American Dance* (Chicago, Illinois: University of Illinois Press, 1996).

Foster, William Patrick, *America's Band of Legend: A Pictorial Collection on Bands at Florida A&M University (1892–1996)* (Tallahassee, Florida: Florida A&M University Bands, 1997).

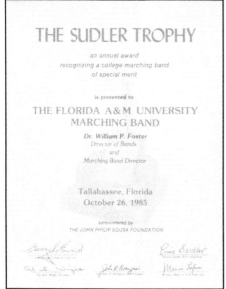

www.ingramcontent.com/pod-product-compliance
Lightning Source LLC
Jackson TN
JSHW011932131224
75386JS00041B/1347

9 7 8 1 5 9 9 3 2 7 2 9 7